Sociological Foundations of Education

Sociological Foundations of Education

HEMLATA TALESRA

KANISHKA PUBLISHERS, DISTRIBUTORS
NEW DELHI-110 002

KANISHKA PUBLISHERS, DISTRIBUTORS
4697/5-21A, Ansari Road, Daryaganj
New Delhi -110 002
Phones : 2327 0497, 2328 8285
Fax : 011-2328 8285
E-mail : kanishka_publishing@yahoo.co.in

Sociological Foundations of Education

First Published: 2002

Edition: 2018

PRINTED IN INDIA

Published by Madan Sachdeva for Kanishka Publishers, Distributors, 4697/5-21A, Ansari Road, Daryaganj, New Delhi-110 002, Typeset by Sunshine Graphics, Delhi, and Printed at Rajdhani Printers, Delhi.

Preface

Education has a fundamental role to play in personal and social development. 21st century dominated by globalisation will bring with it enduring tensions to overcome tensions between the global and the local. The diversity of cultures and system of social organisation is a universal challenge of reinventing the democratic ideal to create or maintain social cohesion.

In order to make India 'acknowledge based society' there is a need to know the society in the educational paraphases. The book 'Sociological Foundation of Education' is trying to analyse different sociological perspectives from educational point of view. The book covers the M.Ed. syllabus of M.S. University, Baroda, CIE: M.L. Sukhadia University Udaipur, Banasthali Deemed University, Agra, Aligarh, Meerut, Ajmer, Jai Narayan Vyas University Jodhpur and Jaipur Universities.

The author that this book will help the M.Ed. students to understand the nature, scope, functions, relationship of educational sociology, sub-systems of Indian society, social stratification and mobility, Social change, equity, universal literacy, politicisation of education, socialistic pattern of society and education, Sociometric study and Social survey.

In the end I express my gratitude to all those authors whose work has inspired me and from whom I had to draw ideas to give more knowledge base subject matter.

I also express my gratitude to Prof. S.L. Doshi a Sociologist, who has been of great help and guidance in planning and organisation of the subject matter.

Hemlata Talesra

Contents

1

Educational Sociology: Concept, Scope, Functions and Relationship Between Educational Sociology and Educational Psychology

Educational sociology is an important division of sociological studies. It makes an effort to achieve the aims of sociology through educational process which occurs between the individual and the society. It is concerned with educational aims, methods, institutions, administration and curricula, in relation to economic, political, religious, social and cultural forces of the society in which they function. In the education of the individual it concerns the influence of social life and social relationships on the development of personality.

Educational sociology may be defined as the application of the scientific spirit, methods and principles of sociology to the study of education. By such study the social laws governing education may be obtained and applied in such ways as will improve our educational practice.

Educational sociology is a new branch of sociology. It was Henry Suzzallo who gave the first courses in Educational Sociology in 1907; the first text being written by Walter R. Smith in 1917. The First *Journal of Educational Sociology* was started in 1927. Then there came the publication of the *Journal of Social Education* in 1936.[1] All this happened in the United States of America.

In India there are some instances of writings which constitute the literature of educational sociology. *The Ashram Vyavstha* was based purely on the tenets of social foundations of society. The *Shastrakars* such as Manu, Vyasa and Valmiki while accepting a person as disciple gave all consideration to the latter's social background. Dronacharya did not accept Eklavya as his disciple for the latter belonged to a Bhil tribe. Similarly, Parashuram rejected Karna when the former came to know of the latter as belonging to the *Kshatriya Varna.* In the ancient Indian educational system, there was no place for women of the untouchables. This could easily be said to be the beginning of the Sociology of Education in India.

But a systematic treatment given to the subject only relates to the later part of the sixties of this century. The studies conducted by I.P. Desai and five other studies by his students mark the beginning of the origin of a scientific approach to the educational sociology in India. The initiative then was taken up by the Education Commission which called together "a group of sociologists to discuss the sociology of education and the immediate contribution sociologists could make in the foundation of Education Policy".[2] The beginning of educational sociology in India indicates the desire of the Government to seek the expertise and confidence of sociologists in the framing of educational policy. As a result of the initiative taken by the government and the favourable response of the sociologists, the problem of 'educational sociology in a modernizing society' was discussed in a seminar in 1964. The deliberations of the seminar are published in a book form.[3] But it should be admitted as has been done by the editors of the book that field data in our country are lacking in respect of the school system. The papers included in the book are, therefore, largely *thematic* in nature. In the field of educational sociology in India, it is a pioneering work indeed.

The essential character of educational sociology is derived from sociology, said otherwise, educational sociology as defined by Cook and Cook[4] is "the application of sociological knowledge and technique to educational problem in the field of human relations and material well-being". Karl Mannhein and Stewart have yet another point to make for defining educational sociology. To them, an enquiry into the sociological foundation of education cannot be purely academic one, pilling up facts for their own sake.[5] There is something definite we want to know. We are in search of something which should never be lost sight of in our research. We want to understand our time, the predicament of this age, what healthy education could contribute to a regeneration of society and man. In this quest for orientation, sociology is a tool and we shall use it in a two-fold sense; as a special theory of education and as a new approach to this history. These two means of access will continually draw upon each other. According to Mannhein and Stewart the utility of sociology for education is to build up a sociological theory of education which can assist us in our present task of winning over the crises.

Burton Clark makes yet another point for Sociology of Education. He says that society and education are inseparable and one who writes a general sociology need understand educational affairs, "who says Society, says Education".[6] According to Clark the perspective of education might construct new frameworks, accumulate data and extend knowledge to illumine the educational condition. In other words, Clark conforms the definition of educational sociology as given by Cook and Cook. It is in the same vein that Robert Stalcup[7] defines educational sociology as, "the application of general principles and findings of sociology to the administration and process of education. This approach attempts to apply principles of Sociology to the instruction of education as a separate social unit."

M.S. Gore and others look the sociology of education from a different perspective. According to them the educational system emerges as a result of the working of differential institutions and this provides an interesting area of analysis to a sociologist. Education as a part of social organism and as such it should be linked with the other sub-systems of the society. Otherwise, education cannot and need not be studied in isolation. Gore and others observe, "The Sociological analysis of any concrete system of education can be conveniently organised along two dimensions—one a discussion of the relationship between the education system and the other segments of the social system, and two, a discussion of the system of education itself."[8]

The discussion on educational sociology thus brings us two basic premises, namely,

1. studies of the educational system as a sub-system of the total system of the society; and

2 the perspectives of sociology are applied in the analysis of educational phenomena.

The definition of sociology of education further involves some conceptual confusion. There are identical terms such as sociology and education, educational sociology and sociological foundations of education, which require a distinct treatment for the sake of clarity.

Educational Sociology: It applies the sociological perspectives for the analysis of educational processes. It is believed that educational sociology is simply the sociological study of education. The application of sociological concepts yields in sights into the understanding of educational problems. It is a two-prong process. On the one hand, it sharpens the sociological conceptualization of tools and techniques, enriches the discipline, and on the other, gives new illumination towards the solution of educational problem.

Sociology of Education: It is an analysis of the sociological processes involved in the educational institutions. Obviously, this area of study emerges from the field of educational sociology and emphasizes the study within the institutions of education.

Social Foundation of Education: This field includes the study of history, philosophy and sociology of education and comparative education. This field is broader than either sociology of education or educational sociology.

The educational sociology after making a study of the interactions of the different elements of the society with the individual throws light on their importance in education. This science emphasizes the progress of the society through the medium of education. The problems of schooling and instructions are looked upon specially as the problems of society. For example, it studies as to what type of education should be given to the children? What should be its curriculum, which books are to be taught and also why the children become delinquents, truants etc.? The answer to these questions can only be obtained through a study of the nature and form of the society. The educational sociology also tries to search a suitable solution of these problems. This science throws light on those institutions and organisations and on those social interactions which are of great importance in educational process. In short, this science utilizes the total educational interaction which helps in the personality development of the individual so that he becomes a better social being.

Scope of Educational Sociology

In Educational sociology we study the educational system as a whole in sociological paraphysis in those areas where the patterns of inter-action are observed. In this respect two models of the major areas of study of educational sociology are important; one model is given by Burton R. Clark[9] and the other one is that of M.S. Gore and others.[10]

Burton Clark while defining the frontiers of sociology of education says that on many a front sociological efforts might construct perspectives, accumulate data and extend knowledge to illumine the educational condition. To be more specific, this brings forth four sectors where sociological enquiry can be fruitful in the study of educational system.

According to Clark the first sector of educational sociology is the education and society. Educational system does not exist in vacuum. It has a definite bearing on the society which possesses it. It is in this sector that sociological enquiry could probe significantly. The relation of economy, social stratification, culture and social integration is closely linked. This education and society interest, becomes world-wide in character as investigation turns to cross-culture comparisons.

The second major and often over-looked sector of sociological attention is the educational institution taken as a whole. As a social institution, education is a web of organisation and associations which is characterised by a growing division of task. It is a labour force, a profession which offers opportunities of recruitment, job status, occupational orientation, mobility and career.

The third sector of sociology of education is the internal life of the educational organisation. It is a potent agency as formal organisation of social change. There is a kind of educational sub-culture which requires to be analysed through sociological frame of reference. The classroom system further constitutes an element of the organisation.

For a fourth sector, sociological enquiry is required to comprehend education outside of education. The growth and spread of educational work is leading to substantial educational sub-systems in the military and in business as well as in the church. The future promises great spread of formal instruction outside of the regular line of schools and colleges and a grasp of the common and uncommon functions of these educational sub-systems would measurably extend understanding of the changing roles of education in the social structure.

The model given by Clark thus consists of the following four sectors or the areas of study for educational sociology:

1. ***Education and Sociology:***

    (*a*) Economy,
    (*b*) Social stratification,
    (*c*) Culture, and
    (*d*) Social Integration.

2. ***Educational Institutions:***

    (*a*) Labour force,
    (*b*) Profession,
    (*c*) Job status,
    (*d*) Occupational orientation,
    (*e*) mobility, and
    (*f*) Career.

3. ***Educational Organisation:***

    (*a*) Formal organisation,
    (*b*) Set of inter-related sub-cultures of students and faculties, and
    (*c*) Teacher-student relationships in classroom situation.

4. ***Educational Sub-systems of Other Institutions:***

    (*a*) Education outside of education,
    (*b*) military,
    (*c*) business, and
    (*d*) church.

In the developing country and more specially in India where efforts are made to bring about induced changes, there have emerged training institutions or institutions of orientation which impart professional skills to personnel to carry on the development work. This is an example of education outside of education. Co-operative colleges, tribal orientation and study centres constitute the extending horizons of education.

M. S. Gore *et al.*, have delineated the scope of sociology of education in India. According to these authors education is a part of the total social system. In their model the first sector of educational sociology, is therefore, education and the social system. Education is related to other aspect of the social system such as kinship, social stratification, political organisation and finally to knowledge and attitude of knowledge. The second sector consists of the education system itself which is a web of the interactions of different statures and roles within the system itself. It includes the organisational pattern of education, teacher-pupil relationship, teacher-administrator relationship, teacher-teacher relationship and student-student interaction.

Looking to the Indian situations, it could be said that the fourth sector of Clark, namely educational sub-systems of other institutions does not find a place in the model of Gore and others. Perhaps, it is due to the fact that in our country not much attention is paid to education in our institutions, such as business and religion, but it cannot be gain said that in a modernizing society education outside of education is bound to gain a significant place. On a broader plane, it could be said that educational sociology employs all the major perspectives and conceptual frames of sociology in analysing the education system and its relationship with the total social system. According to Dr. S. S. Mathur[11] the specific problems which are vital organs in its study are as follows:

1. What is the importance of teacher in the society and how can he be given a place of honour in it?
2. What type of relationship should be established between the teacher and the taught? How do social feelings influence this relationship?
3. How can mutual relationships be established between school and other agencies?
4. What are the needs and the motives of the local community?
5. How can social elements be broken in smaller units like school, play group etc. and what relationships do exist between them?
6. How does the social life influence the school and the individual?
7. How can through ideal social life and good schooling democratic feelings be inculcated?
8. How can such desirable changes in the curriculum which may help in the progress of the individual and the society be brough about?

9. What is the importance of press, radio and films in the sociological process?
10. How are the social progress and social control possible?

In this way, we can say that in the scope of educational sociology the study of each and every type of social relationship is included.

Functions of Educational Sociology

The structure and functions of educational sociology varies very much with the goals of a society. A. H. Halsey has laid down two major functions of educational sociology for a technological society.[12]

1. The survival of a society depends on the persistence of its cultural patterns, traditions, beliefs and skills. These cultural phenomena are not carried in the genetic constitution of individuals. There is need to learn the culture. Thus the prime function of educational sociology is that of cultural transmission.
2. The society wants to maintain its equilibrium, in parsonian terms, the pattern maintenance. It is realised when its members "fit" into the cultural setting of the society. Educational sociology, therefore, has another function of the formation of social personalities. By transmitting the culture through appropriate molding of social personalities, education in sociological paraphyses contributes to the integration of the society as a mechanism that enables men to adopt themselves to their environment, to survive and to reproduce themselves.

Education in sociological terms, therefore, is a potential agency of socialisation and acquisition of power. The Indian society which has passed through various stages has now received some salient features. We want to achieve in the light of the new values, norms and goals given by the constitution, legislation, state policies and Five Year Plans. Such a portrait of Indian society would help us to analyse the responsibilities of education for training the members of the society.

The Indian Constitution in its Fundamental Rights has given "Seven Freedoms" to a citizen. These freedoms or rights are contained in Part III of the Indian Constitution. Accordingly the Individual has right to equality and a right against exploitation.

The freedom to property which is given to the individual gives Indian society a form of a capitalist society. The Fundamental Rights can be acquired through Constitutional remedies. This is a significant factor towards holding the Indian society as a capitalist society. Yet another special feature of the society is that the Constitution bestows a secular way of life on its citizens in religion, culture and language. This pluralistic nature of Indian society has tended to make it a multi-lingual society. Such a society presupposes an inherent conflict, at least for a transitory period, between pluralism or regionalism and nationalism. The values and norms given by the Constitution are based on humanism and rationality. One of the function of Education Sociology is to provide knowledge and solution of the values, norms and the conflicts of society.

Nowhere the Constitution gives an outline of Indian society. Neither the Five Year Plans make any effort in this direction though the Parliament passed a Bill in 1954 to achieve a socialistic pattern of society. The Congress ruling party has passed a resolution in its Bombay session to strive to achieve a democratic socialist society. On the basis of such pronouncements made from time to time and review of the Constitution, Five Year Plans and Government policies, a tentative outline of the nature of Indian social order which is the main function of Educational Sociology. Educational Sociology provides knowledge, skill and quality which are essential for the adjustment in the new social order. The characteristics of new social order are given below:

1. *Harmonious Order:* We want to achieve a social order where there are minimum of unequalities. Ascriptive social differentiation needs to be ousted. Negatively, the society would be excluded of class conflict, exploitation, unequal rights and privileges and wide decentralization of economic and political power.

2. *Changing Society:* We have adopted science and technology as our constant companions. A technological society presupposes constant change. It is said that in the present world scientific knowledge gets two-fold within a decade. A single technology has a life of about seven years. In such a rapidly changing situation of science and technology, the society that we want to achieve would be a fast moving society. Modernisation is a process which involves industrialisation, urbanisation, and rationalisation, as a principle process to bring about this change in the society. Commenting on the role of modernisation in Indian society Yogendra Singh observes: "Modernism and industrial society would represent the culture

and social structure respectively which India today aspires for. Modernity consists of values of humanism, pragmatism and relativism. Democracy, rational administration (bureaucracy), large scale production through higher technology and science are some of the structural prototypes which synchronise with the value system of modernity."[13] The dominance of science, technology and rationality involves discontinuity with old habit, customs and traditions. Sociology of education introduces the technological development and social change and help to maintain the pattern of society.

3. ***Rising Standard of Living:*** In the future form of society the life style of the members has to rise rapidly. The old tradition or the tradition propounded by Mahatma Gandhi that of the state of wantlessness does not find any place in this scheme of society.

4. ***Mixed Economy:*** The Government has made two polar categories of economy—free economy and state enterprise. Exclusive state enterprise tends to render the Government as a socialist state and an exclusive free economy makes the country capitalist. The public sector and the private sector has two dichotomies of our economy work as a model and regulator.

5. ***Equal Opportunities:*** The society would provide equal opportunities to all. One of the strongest means of providing opportunities and equality is the education of different types organised by state devices.

6. ***Comprehensive Development:*** The Constitution provides safeguards for all sections of the society. The different walks of life—from folklore to politics—receive the developmental efforts of the Government. Development in this sense would remain an idiom of Indian society. But little or no assumption is made in this regard to the transformation of patterns of values in the process of the implementation of plan.

7. ***Democratic Process:*** The society would achieve its rational goals by employing democratic processes, "It is based on the effective power of the active co-operation of citizens." It has an efficient administrative setup. Freedom in the expression of opinion is assumed.

8. ***Pluralistic—Multilingual Society:*** The term of society would consist of the pluralistic existence of different subcultures. It also expects the operationality of national languages. The society would have its integration in territorial borders and in economy and politics.

In other aspects the society would enjoy a pluralistic—regional—lingual identity.

*9. **Welfare State:*** The state is a welfare one. It is dynamic and is to be primarily supplied by the growth of community feeling, co-operative habits of action and social education, on the one hand, and simultaneous economic and social development under central direction, guidance and control, on the other.

*10. **Urban Nature:*** As a result of the acceptance of science and technology, the resultant social structure would be largely urban-oriented. In the decades to come the villages as we know them today would cease to have existence. They would become small urban centres.

The image of society that we want to build is not a dream of Utopia. Actually the image that is manifest in various pronouncements and policies consists of the goals that we have set for achievement. The realisation of the kind of socialistic society makes it obligatory for an effective performance of various roles. There is a close relationship between individual socialisation and social consensus. The main function of education in sociological perspective is to form personalities which embody the challenges given by the society.

The design of Indian society clearly indicates that in future science and research would achieve an institutional form. We would have to develop and would become part of a complex technology. Educational sociology will help to face the complex situation of the society.

We have sketched a bench-mark of Indian society that we want to build or achieve. The bench-mark, may be admitted, does not exist in reality. It is neither a description of actual society. Educational sociology in this regard perform functions and help in a planned way to move towards this direction of socialistic society.

Talcott Parsons mentioned in his book; "The School Class as a Social System: Some of its Functions in American Society" has said an industrial-urban society education has to perform two functions:

1. Socialisation, and
2. Selection.

Education has to develop (a) Commitments, and (b) capacities in the process of development. In a developing society the individual has to commit himself to the common values and norms of the society. And then his further commitment is towards the performance of the specialised roles assigned to him. It is usually in the occupation. Thus socialisation in the field of commitment has to take two forms:

(*a*) commitment to values,
(*b*) commitment to the performance of specialised roles.

The main function of education is to impart skills necessary to perform the roles. This involves usually the acquisition of technical roles. Secondly, education helps the individual to develop capacities for carrying out the role, responsibility and the expectations of his group. Obviously, this part of capacities refers to the social development of the individual.

The second, function of education in sociological perspective given by persons is selection. It means "allocation of human resources within the role structure of the adult society."[14] The individual in an industrial society has voluntaristic mode of action where he has to depend on selectivity of different roles.

Functions of Education as Socialising Agent

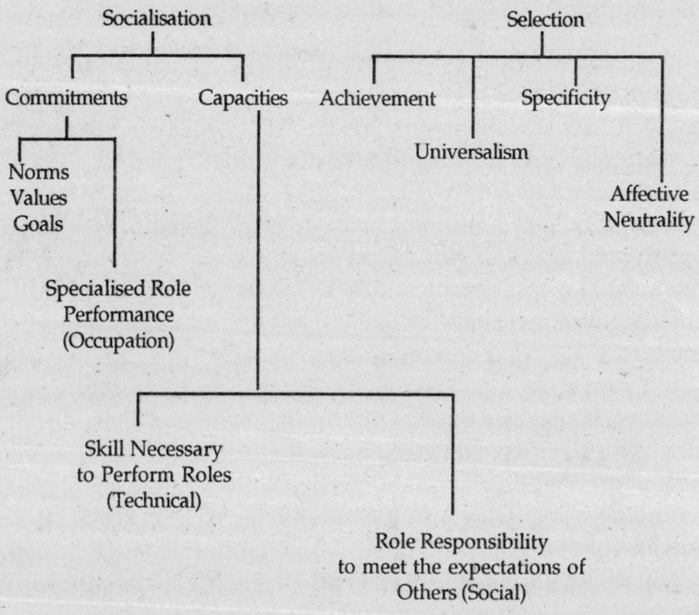

In a complex role society that India endures to achieve education has to train persons for effective selection of different kinds of roles. The society now has taken a new model which prescribes the role—sets charged with the values of achievement, universalism, specificity and effective neutrality. In such a situation of planned and committed society the role of education, therefore, assumes a significant importance. There is mass illiteracy in the country. New specialised jobs are increasingly emerging and education has to impart knowledge to its incumbents in regard to the socialisation of commitments and capacities and prepares them for voluntaricism.[15] The role that education has to play in our present society in sociological paraphrase can be sketched on page 12.

The newly envisaged scientific order of society has widely affected the structure of educational system. Educational system refers to the major institutions, associations and personnel for formal or school as opposed to familial education, whose end is the conversion of social neonates into full-fledged citizen. Educational Sociology in the present context as a variant process of modernisation is confronted with two problems: On the one hand, it has to maintain the core values and, on the other, to introduce the values of secularism and rationality in the Indian society.[16]

Relationship Between Educational Psychology and Educational Sociology

A society is a group of intelligent beings possessing conscious likeness and acting together on the basis of common interests. It is composed of individual associating with one-another in some sort of group relationships. To be properly understood it must be studied from both the individual and the social point of view, and the results harmonised. The study of nature has developed a number of sciences which overlap but whose boundaries have become fairly well marked. The study of man has likewise developed a variety of sciences but the phenomena are so complex that their boundaries are less clearly delimited. This is particularly true in the social sciences and there is even more frequent clashing over the fields of sociology and psychology.

The fundamental distinction is sufficient to clear the subjects. Sociology is properly concerned with man only in his social aspects, while psychology, in his individual aspects. The primary interest of sociology is in the study of social relations, while the primary interest of psychology is in the study of individual mental life. The unit of study of sociology is, therefore, the social group, while that of psychology the individual man. Thus sociology approaches the study of the individual through society while psychology approaches the study of society through the individual. Psychology studies the human life and behaviour. Whatever influences are exercised by heredity and environment on the individual are discussed and analysed by psychology. It studies the instincts, general innate tendencies, laws of heredity, emotions etc. Besides this it endeavours to know the influence of unconscious on personality. On the basis of this wholesome knowledge educational psychology tries to make the learning process easier and healthy. Educational psychology explains as to under what conditions education and instruction can best be given.

Educational sociology emphasises the social elements in the learning process. In this way, both the subjects gave importance to education and instruction. Both the subjects throw light on the development of personality of the individual. Psychology tries to understand the human personality by making a study of conscious and unconscious elements while educational sociology makes a study of human personality through sociological point of view.[17] From a broader point of view there is not much difference between sociology and psychology since the main subject of study of both these disciplines is human being himself. The modern educational psychology studies the social environment found in family, school and society. Under the scope of this subject alone comes the study of unconscious mind, the nature urges, drives and innate tendencies which influence the behaviour of the individuals. It also throws light on habits, learning attitudes, aptitudes, character, motivation etc. The educational sociology gains very much from this knowledge. The psycho-analysts have shown how greatly the unconscious have shown, how greatly the unconscious of an individual influences the development of his personality. It is not possible to understand the nature of the society and to keep a control over it unless a study is made of the inner mental make-up of the individuals. To study unconsciousness is not the task of educational sociology but it is an important study in the field of psychology. Therefore, sociology seeks the help of psychology in understanding the unconscious mind and its function. It is on account of this factor that they are so close.

Educational sociology through psychological methods studies the nature of the society and the interaction of the individual with the society. Thus psychology is an important instrument for the study of educational sociology.

In pursuing his researches the sociologist cannot overlook the nature of the individual in determining society, nor can the Psychologist neglect the influence of society in forming the individual. Hence, there arises a debatable ground dealt with by both sociologists and psychologists and known as "Social Psychology" or "Psychological Sociology". Aside from this limited area, the field of the two sciences are clearly marked and their applications are certainly broad enough and important enough to need all of the energy each can give to his own field.

References

1. Lloyd Allen Cook and Elaive Farsyth Cook, *A Sociological Approach to Education* (2nd ed.), McGraw Hill Company, N.Y. 1950, p. 9.
2. Gore, M.S. and Others, *Papers in the Sociology of Education in India* (eds.), National Council of Educational Research and Training, 1967, pp. V-VI.
3. *Ibid.*
4. Lloyd Allen Cook and Elaive Farsyth Cook: *Ibid.*
5. Mannhein, Karl and Wac Stewart, *An Introduction to the Sociology of Education*, Routledge & Kegan Paul, London, 1964 (2nd Imp.) p. 160.
6. Clerk, Burton R., "Sociology of Education", *Handbook of Modern Sociology*, Robert B. L., Raris (ed.), Rand Mcnally and Co., Chicago, p. 7656.
7. Stalcup, Robert J., *Sociology and Education*, Charles E. Merrill Publishing Company, Columbia, Ohio, 1968, p. 5.
8. Gore, M.S. and Others: *Ibid.*
9. Clerk Burton: *Ibid.*
10. Gore and Others: *Ibid.*, pp. V-VI.
11. Mathur, Dr. S. S., *A Sociological Approach to Indian Education*, Vinod Pusthak Mandir, Agra, Third edition, 1973, p. 36.
12. Halsey, A. H., "The Sociology of Education", *The Sociology*, Neil J. Smelser (ed.), John Wiley and Sons, New York, 1967, p. 385.
13. Yogendra Singh, "The Process of Socialisation and Education", Papers in the *Sociology of Education in India* (ed.) M. S. Gore, NCERT, New Delhi, 1967.

14. Parsons, Talcott, *The School Class as a Social System: Some of its Functions in American Society*, Free Press, USA, 1951.
15. *Ibid.*
16. Ottaway, A.K.C. "The Aim and Scope of Educational Sociology" *Educational Review*, Vol. 12, No. 3, June 1960.
17. Anthony Leeds, "Cultural Factors in Education: India, Brazil, The United States, The Soviet Union, some problems of Applied Anthropology," *Contemporary Indian*, Baidyanath Verma, ed, Asia Publishing House, Bombay, 1964, p. 273.

2

Indian Social Structure: Its Nature

The social structure of traditional Indian society was based mainly on the hereditary principle. The members were divided into hereditary caste-groups each with its traditional occupation, therefore, was a ascribed to him by society. In the ancient period of Indian history it was a means for the attainment of the spiritual goal of self-realization mostly through self introspection (*uddharet atmanah atmenam*) by renunciation of worldly pursuit in a social living. The actions of the individual in this society were inherently structured on a normative, teleological socio-cultural group pattern. The normative structure consisted of *purushartha-Dharm, Artha, Kama* and *Moksha.* A person in this scheme of life was expected to behave in a normative orientation of a religious sect and caste and achieve the goal of self-realization. This ideology of Indian society was followed in the ancient period up to the period of the synthesis in the *Geeta,* the *Smritis* and *Arthashastra.*[1] This was, in fact, the model of *Sanatan Dharm,* the eternal religion.

The Indian Constitution now upholds the democratic principle of social organisation. Democracy stands for some kind of equality among individuals. Social equality may be broadly divided into two types, equality of conditions and equality of opportunities. The main aim of democracy is limited towards securing equality of opportunity whereby persons should receive social rights and privileges according to their capacity, ability and function.

The main aspects of social structure of Indian society are the caste and the class systems:

1. Caste System: Caste system may be defined as the integration of interacting endogamous group into a structure of status hierarchy. In the traditional Indian society, a community was divided into a number of endogamous groups of inter-marrying circles called castes. Members in each caste group followed the same hereditary occupation and were socio-economically homogenous. These groups were graded in a hierarchy of social prestige. The caste stratification is found even now in almost every Indian community defined in terms of locality, but the degree of its rigidity varies from community to community. Even today caste is an institution of great strength and considered as an important component of the social structure of a village.

2. Class System: The class system, on the other hand may be described as the division of society into different prestige category or classes. Usually, it is the prestige of the occupations followed by person which determine their position in the class system irrespective of the castes to which they belong.

3. Family: Family is a group where man and woman live together in a socially accepted relationship. The family socializes the children and impart them the value patterns of the society. It gives elementary forms of behaviour to its wards. In the context of modernizing Indian society, the institution of family has received new horizons. The forces of modernization have tended to break the traditional Indian joint family. The rural families still tread on the traditional path, but if the forces of modernity continue to operate effectively, the family structure in this area would also change.

4. Religion: There is no country in the world where religion plays an important part in the daily life of the people, then it does in India. It not only usher them through the great events of earthly existence: birth, marriage and death and fixed their position in the social scale, but it even decides what they may eat and drink, who may prepare their food and when it is awful for them to be shaved.

In a broad sense, religious outlook on life is the same as spiritual outlook. In India, religion does not appear to the people to be merely a set of intellectual beliefs. With an attitude of comprehensive spirituality, instead of an inflexible creed, the Hindu religious outlook has accepted this multiplicity of aboriginal gods and others and justified them all, thus bringing together into one whole all believers in the religious spiritualistic theme of life.

The religious concepts in varied forms determine the social structure of the different regions of India, presenting to the anthropologist a picture of cultural diversity. The attitude of spiritual and religious outlook gives in social link within and between villages in India.

*5. **Pluralism:*** The attitude of pluralism may be traced to the ontological make-up of the Hindu world-view. It is a method of allowing each individual or group to get to truth in his own tradition by means of disciplines of mind and morals. The Bhagwad Gita calls it *'Swadharma'*. Nothing is good which is not self-chosen and no determination is valuable which is not self-determination.

In another pluralism is the value of adjustment to the pluralistic reality. As Dube points out,[2] "the fundamental drive in the thought and activities of the group seems to be towards the goal of adjustment of the individual to the universe".

The theme of pluralism in Indian culture is borne out from historical necessity and has strong bases in the Hindu religious practices and is supported by Hindu ontology. Apart from the polytheistic manifestations this configuration of values expresses in the life of an average Indian the following cluster of values:

1. Multiplicity of approaches to social problems as a social value.
2. Tolerance as a valued concept both in religious and secular life.
3 Unity in diversity as an underlying value, current alongwith pluralistic approach.
4. Swadharma as a directional value toward self-chosen and self-determined religious and social behaviour within the limitation of unity in diversity.
5. Adjustment as a value leading to non-controlling the universe but toward establishing a passive balanced reordering of the environment.

Inter-Relationship Between the Structures

India is a multi-racial, multi-religious, multi-caste, multi-lingual and multi-cultural country. The pages of history are full of the fragrance of communal harmony as well as the venom of communal discord. Contrary to expectations of our national leaders who waged the struggle for freedom, the post-Independence era of our country has been innumerable communal riots and endless quarrels and tensions of various issues like state-boundaries language, establishment of a mill or dam in one's state, atrocities, on scheduled castes or a minority community etc. A keen observer of the Indian society, Prof. M. N. Srinivas correctly reports:[3]

> "India is not only vast and culturally and religiously diverse but its population is also very sharply stratified, socially as well as economically. A crucial consequence of the divisions which characterise Indian society everywhere is widespread 'minority consciousness. . . ."

Different terms related to social structure such as 'caste', 'class', 'family', 'village', 'community' and 'kinship' are defined as segmentary entities. On the basis of the study of K.S. Singh the integration of caste is into the class. Transformation of the caste is due to current changes that are taking place in the wider society. Surjit Sinha had delineated the process of assimilation of caste into class peasant base of Indian civilization through the adoption of agricultural technology and linguistic and cultural norms.

G. S. Aurora, who has worked among the Bhils and Bhilas, of the region of Alirapur in the district of Jhabua of Madhya Pradesh discusses the trend of social change among the tribals. He proposes his thesis in terms of tribe-caste-class social formation. Putting his findings he observes:[4]

> This appers to be particularly true of the ritual relations between the two landowning Jatis—Bhils and Bhilas—who act towards each other almost as equals; whereas the rituals of social relations between these land-owning *Jati* and Belais—who own very little land do follow the 'caste pattern' somewhat rigorously.

Further, Haimendort advances the thesis that in the process of social formation there is a move among the caste people to the status. D. N. Majumdar[5] envisages three stages in the process of sanskritisation among the Garos. In the first stage the tribals give up "unclean habits like beef eating, keeping of pigs and fowls or the eating of pork and fowl. Both of these is a sign that the tribe wants acceptance in Hindu society and a claim to belong. Second, is the abandonment of tribal deities and rites from the Hindu pantheon and the celebration of ceremonies associated with Hindu deities. These would now be performed by a Brahman priest. The third stage being relinquishing of clan organization and replacing it by Hindu clan system. To crown the entire process, Majumdar hints that the adoption of an Aryan language would complete de-tribalization in its totality.

Most of the tribals and other backward castes are affected by technological change. Those who live in or near the city of Jamshedpur are especially apt to part of the working force in the steel mills there. Schermerhorn[6] who has analysed the multiplicity of Indian ethnicity, argues that the people of different castes have taken different dimension of social formation. A segment of people persues to attain caste status for improving their rank. Concluding his findings the author says that the transition from caste to class takes many forms and may often remain at an intermediate stage for decades or generations.

The argument that the family and caste people are changing into class is contested by a large number of social scientists. They also argue that the process of social formation is heavily influenced by the attainment of varying educational standards. Those who propagate the hypothesis that the people are changing from caste to class obviously have a Marxist perspective.

The political and economic process of social transformation have created a secular society as a result of change they are not integrating themselves from any caste or class. His observations very clearly indicate that the forces of education and economic modernisation have changed the direction of social change among the people. They are moving from caste to class agricultural labourers, wage earners, factory workers, officers, administrators, educationists etc. The emerging pattern of people's polity presents heterogenous way of integration. The peasants who have acquired landed property and better means of production are united with the upper strata of regional society through the capitalist market, money, education and competitive politics. Another group belonging to landless peasantry or wage earners have united with the lower strata of the wider society. The national model remains the ideal for both the strata of the society.

Problems of Indian Society in the Context of National Development

The problem of Indian society in the context of national development is complicated. India's history, its geography and its heritage—racially, linguistically and culturally have made the country diverse in habits, customs, thought and other aspects of living. Basic to the analysis of this problem is the identification of the heritage of India in its two antecedental areas; namely,

1. the heritage of conflicts in its religious, linguistic, economic, political and cultural dimensions, and
2. the heritage of cultural unity in its projective and maintenance dimensions.

The most characteristic feature of the Indian civilization is the processes by which diverse elements are related to one-another to form the civilization, therefore, the problem of national development in India ought to be seen against the characteristic diversification.

Racial Problem: The people of India can be viewed as essentially made of six racial groups occupying specific blocks of territory.[7]

1. Indo-Aryan (Punjab, Rajputana and Kashmir)
2. Saytho-Dravidian (Gujarat, Bombay)
3. Aryo-Dravidian (Uttar Pradesh, Eastern Rajputana, Bihar)
4. Mongolo-Dravidian (Bengal, Coastal Orissa)
5. Mongoloid type (Himachal Pradesh, Assam, Nepal, Bhutan, Sikkim), and
6. Dravidian (Madras, Andhra, Kerala, Madhya Pradesh, Highland Orissa, Mysore).

The student of social sciences in India does come across the problem of professed beliefs of racial superiority and inferiority in certain situations of difference in the country. Though colour has not been associated as a distinguishing feature of any group of people, a certain type of 'shade-complex' is identifiable in the social relations of people, which is some times traced to racial characteristics of a family or a group. The fairer shade of a person is at times attributed to the person's of Aryan origin and the darker shades are attributed to the Dravidian stock. Such beliefs in the origin of colour shades of people quite often lead to social discrimination with its concommitant hostilities of mutual groups. Similarly, the hierarchical positions of castes are also believed to have their origin in the racial characteristics. The Brahmins and other higher castes believe themselves to be of the Aryan race and those of the lower castes of the Dravidian race.

Problem of Maintaining Secular States

In India the meaning of inter-cultural education has to be consistent with the ideals of democratic pluralism, upheld by the Indian Constitution, which are:

> "JUSTICE—social, economic and political; LIBERTY of thought, expression, belief, faith and worship, EQUALITY of status and opportunity; and to promote among them all FRATERNITY assuring the dignity of the individual and the unity of nation.[8]

In other words, inter-cultural education in India has to be based upon five basic principles:

1. Every individual in India has a deserving and destiny of his own.
2. Society exists for the individual and not the individual for the society.
3. Equality and majority rule ought to work in a mutually supplementing and not in supplanting manner.
4. Discrimination on grounds of religion, race, caste, sex or language is repugnant to societal living.
5. Every group in India has a right to protect, conserve and promote its own culture.

The principles derived from the Indian Constitution imply that differences in ideology and cultural patterns that characterize groups should be tolerated and honoured. Therefore, the scope of intercultural education in India should embrace much more than instilling love and regard for one's own sub-culture or a measure of respect for members of their sub-cultures. It should include the formation of an intellectual understanding and appreciation of the real purpose, ideals and contributions of all sub-cultures, be they religious, linguistic or socio-economic. Particular attention has to be obviously given to groups which may not come within the conventional framework of the majority of the dominant group in a societal situation.

Some Indologists feel that Democracy as a value is a part of the traditional heritage of India. It is supposed to have been operating and guiding the lives of people in their working of village republics from time immemorial. Examples of the behaviour of kings like Rama are quoted from the epics to show how the king respected the common man's opinion about his own conduct and how the king decided even to send away his dear wife to the forest to respect public opinion. But whatever may be the force of these isolated instances in the epics of India, one would hesitate to assume the operation of democracy to educate the people of India for an enduring national solidarity. In India there is a problem of maintaining secular state. In fact, secularism is often referred to as a qualification to Indian democracy, in order to provide greater universality and of religious-cum-spiritual attitudes. It is even regarded as the main force of commonality in the country, in view of the recent communal history and the varied religious groups that are effectively operating in the body politic today. The people of India have accepted the theme of secularism as a guiding value, but there can be little doubt that in public life and organisational activities not merely the Indian Constitution has given an unambiguous directive.

It may also be pointed out that verbalizations and to some extent adherence to the theme of secularism have become emotionally charged in certain sections of the national body politic. After the bitter experience of partition of the country, based on religious minority claims and after Pakistan has adopted a theoratic Constitution, the importance of the theme of secularism has greatly increased and the people and the body politic react sharply against non-secular elements of the country.

Upholding Democratic Principles

Article 46 of the Indian Constitution lays down the following directive principles in regard to social justice,

> "The State shall promote with special care the educational and economic interests of the weaker sections of the people and in particular of the Scheduled Castes and the Scheduled Tribes and shall protect them from social unjustice and all forms of exploitation."

The concept of social Justice as enunciated by the above directive principle has led to many voluntary organisations formed on caste basis to safeguard the interests of the members of their respective castes. Under the context of democracy, these organisations assume a political power in the caste society, in the country in view of the traditional values.

The greatest force of modern Indian democracy is the spirit and provisions of the Indian Constitution. Progressively, the theme of democracy is tending to become more and more comprehensive in its scope and application in the country. Probably, the most significant introduction into the lives of Indian citizens is the recent attempts of the government of the country to effect Panchayati Raj, or progressive democratic decentralization in the sphere of local government. A study of the contemporary events in Indian social and political life indicates a strong trend towards the theme of democracy percolating down to the bases of Indian culture and therefore, it has to be a great unifying force in the country today.

Linguistic Diversities

One of the most dividing features of Indian national life today is the situation of difference caused by the languages. Although, there are many bilingual and multilingual groups in the country, it is possible to classify the people of India into distinct language groups where one or the other of Indian language is dominantly spoken by the people of the area. In India there are about 845 languages or dialects including 720 Indian languages spoken by less than a lakh of persons each and 63 non-Indian languages. The people of India may be broadly divided into four linguistic groups, namely, the Indo-Aryan, the Dravidian, the Austro-Asiatic and the Sino-Tibetan-Indo-Aryan languages are divisible at lower levels into dialects of colloquial forms, which Gumperz calls a regional standard. For example, Bihari is divided into three regional standards, namely, Bhojpuri, Maithili and Magadhi. Similarly, Marathi is divisible into Desi and Konkani and so on.

Dravidian language include 11 distinct languages, namely Tamil, Telugu, Kannada, Malyalam, Kodagu, Gond, Khond, Oraoh and Rajmahal.

The Austro-Asiatic languages which are spoken by over 50 lakhs of people include Santhali, Mundari, Ho, Khasi, and Nicobarese.

The Sino-Tibetan, languages are used by small groups of Indians living along the southern slopes of the Himalayas in North Bengal and Assam. The principal languages of this group are Newari and Meithai.[9]

Besides these main four linguistic groups, there are 63 non-

Indian languages spoken by Indians. Chief of them are English, Persian, Chinese, Arabic, Burmese, Portuguese, French and so on.

Thus in India there are literally hundreds of linguistic groups each with its own characteristic sub-culture. However, 97 per cent of the Indian population fall under one or the other of the fourteen major linguistic classification as mentioned, in the 8th schedule of the Indian Constitution. The linguistic distance between Hindi and the other languages left a social cleavage between the northern and the southern parts of India and a feeling of being handicapped for effective citizenship in the country among the people.

The varieties of Indian languages pose situation of difference in the Indian social life. As Karve points out that in all discussions of regionalism either political or cultural language has been a consistent and prime factor in India.[10]

Piuralistic Nature of Indian Social Structure

The pluralistic approach to life and the world may be considered as emanating from the religious and spiritual theme. The attitude of pluralism may be traced to the ontological make up of the Hindu world-view. As Dr. S. Radhakrishnan pointed out "He whose consciousness is anchored in God cannot deny any expression of life as utterly erroneous". He is convinced of the inexhaustability of the nature of God and the infinite number of its manifestations.[11] Consciousness of self cannot fully come by reasoning of the intellect since regarding the external objects, the discursive intellect can confine itself only to discernible aspects. This ontological faith ingrained in the life of a Hindu enables him to have a plurality of approaches to the socio-economic and even religious matters. It is the faculty of observing an object or a problem from several points at the same time which distinguishes the Indian mind from the western mind.

The pluralistic orientation takes the form of diverse cultural attitude and behaviours which may be categorically divided into the sub-values. Tolerance is an important value that emanates from this theme. The way in which judicial affairs are conducted in Village Panchayats illustrates this point. The anti-social elements are dealt with in a way so as to re-establish order rather than punish the offender for its own sake. The right way to refine the crude beliefs and actions, says a popular proverb in Kannada, is to alter the bias of the mind, for what counts is conduct and not belief. The acceptance of the innumerable gods and religious practices allowing them to exist alongside a highly intellectual type of faith without emphasizing conversion of the one into the other, highlights this value in Indian society.

Pluralism is only a method of allowing each individual or group to get to truth in his own tradition by means of discipline of mind and morals. The Bhagwad Gita calls this *'Swadharma'*. Nothing is good which is not self chosen and no determination is valuable which is not self-determination. It is in effect a greater emphasis on the means rather than on the end.

Another sub-value emanating from them of pluralism is the value of adjustment to the pluralistic reality. As Dube pointed out "the fundamental drive in the thought and activities of the group seems to be towards the goal of adjustment of the individual to the Universe."[12]

When we think about the theme of pluralism in Indian culture, it may be noted that this theme is born out of historical necessity and has strong bases in the Hindu religious practices and is supported by Hindu ontology. Apart from the polytheistic manifestations this configuration of values expresses in the life of the average Indian the following cluster of values:

1. Multiplicity of approaches to social problems as a social value.
2. Tolerance as a valued concept both in religion and secular life.
3. Unity in diversity as an underlying value, current along with pluralistic approach.
4. Swadharma as a directional value towards self-chosen and self-determined religious and soical behaviour within the limitation of unity in diversity.
5. Adjustment as a value leading to non-controlling the universe but towards establishing a passive balance recording of the environment.

Role of Education for National Development

In Indian society today, it has been pointed out that there are fundamental changes taking place in social conditions and patterns of life and bases of power. New institutions are springing up and a new hope and aspiration for better living have been generated. But the restless society finds itself unprepared to grasp the new spirit so that it steadily rise alongwith them. Either the people want to get the benefits of the new age too soon or they feel themselves lost in the sweeping changes that are made in those that remain from an earlier pattern of culture. Thus the stability of society is affected and forces of disunity are showing up.

The remedy for this malady is the education of the young and a re-education of old. The lag between the aspirations of the people and their preparedness to use and create resources to achieve them, in making the people to stick to the familiar and look for immediate individual gains, resulting in the reinforcement of the regional loyalties and situations of widening differences between the subcultures. Our attitudes and understandings reflect an age that is gone.

The earth in the meanwhile has become a little neighbourhood. The impact of foreign cultures has assumed gigantic proportions. Retreat into the past has become impossible. Perpetuation of the present is dangerous. So, the only rationale course open to the country's survival is to build on the existing material foundations a comparable superstructure of social institutions and create an appropriate climate of opinion, of concepts and of moral that will open up 'new horizons in India', so the 'future will fascinate her far more than the immediate past of frustrations and humiliations. Here lies the role of education for national development.

The tradition of education as it is functioning today is one of the conservation and transmission of our heritage, importation and inculcation of foreign ideas and techniques and thus preparing the people to be fed on consumer education on these remains of foreign harvests. A new orientation to our education has therefore become a must and the new education has to be more engaged in interpreting the future and encouraging innovations for the future than transmitting the past; education has to help in developing ideas and techniques within the country and make the nation self-sustaining.

In the light of the above frame of reference the following steps focusses on the role of education in bringing about understanding and promotion of educational development in India.

It must be stated at the very outset that education is inherently an integrating tool. This is not to say that the educated people do not contribute to national disunity. But education in a country which is eighty per cent literate has the tremendous potentiality of creating an equality of opportunity and of cutting across the traditional, rigid caste-like stratifications in society. In fact, providing a mobility potential to a caste-ridden society is both a qualitative and a quantitative role of education in a traditional society. It is interesting to refer hereto a research study on the rural expectations of a Telangana village in which the people of the village appear to have indicated three major expectations from the educational activities of the government in that village. They were the expectations of getting a job to improve the family economy, of reducing the population pressure on family lands and of securing a tool for survival and adjustment in the changing democratic society.[12] It is obvious from the above study that even the people feel that education provides a scope for improving their economic and social position. This potentiality of education cannot be overemphasized in the present situation of conflict obtainable in the country due to economic and social inequalities.

Providing compulsory, universal and useful education may therefore, be mentioned as the first step towards building nationhood. Obviously, this step meets with the problem of special endeavour to educate the traditionally backward parts of the society in the context of Constitutional directive of social justice.

Backward and scheduled castes in Indian society have traditionally been neglected in so far as the provision for economic and social growth is concerned. This situation has led to a considerable amount of hostilities between what may be called the 'forward' and the 'backward' communities of the Indian society. Merely providing an equality of educational opportunity to all classes of people in India, may therefore, be considered inadequate to tackle the traditional conflicts between the privileged and non-privileged communities. There is no doubt that national integration by the process of education will be incomplete without an attempt to raise the economic and educational levels of some sections of the society who are kept at a backward level for centuries by traditions of the Indian society. How best to provide an equality of educational opportunity taking into consideration the existing social injustice and the educability of people, is a delicate attempt to build the foundation of national education on which alone the superstructure of national development can rest.

India is not a homogenous society. There are within the vast mass of the Indian population, distinct groups and sub-cultures, who differ from each other in major aspects of their living. Education and its concommitant, equality of opportunity may not round off the angularities of these sub-cultures and may on the other hand even reinforce or sharpen the inter-group differences by generating aspirations of deriving group advantages in the present situation of discrepancies between resources and aspirations.[14]

Under the present conditions of democratic pluralism the only alternative to national development among the different sub-cultures of the nation.[15] From this point of view education assumes an inevitable and a great responsibility to effect the development of the nation.

In India, the national development has to be based on sounder foundations of cross-cultural understanding and appreciation, rather than on sentimental attachments to one's own glory of the heritage of ones own culture. From this point of view, researches and studies in India on inter-cultural understanding and inter-group education are a greater necessity for effecting national development than sentimental approaches of making all the children in schools to sing the national antheme. We wish to suggest that attempts should be made in India to provide an understanding of inter-cultural differences and commonality among the different sub-cultures and evolve techniques of group living and action in the schools, colleges, based upon objective and scientific investigation in the social foundations of education.[16] Inter-cultural education is taken to mean instruction and training designed to promote better understanding and improved human relationships among individuals of many sub-cultural groups.

References

1. Whitehead Henry (1924), *Indian Problems in Religion, Education, Politics,* Constable and Co. Ltd., London.
2. Dube, S.C. (1955), *Indian Village,* Cornell University Press, Ithaca,
3. Srinivas, M. N. (1966), *Social change in Modern India;* Allied Pub., Bombay.
4. Arora, G.S. (1972), *Tribe, Caste and Class Encounters,* Administrative Staff College of India, Hyderabad.
5. Majumdar, D.N. (1969), "A Study of Tribe-Caste Continum and the process of Sanskritisation Among the Bodo-Speaking Tribes of the Garo Hills", *Tribal Situation in India,* Simla.

6. Shermerhorn, R.A., (1978), *Ethnic Plurality in India*, University of Arizona Press, Tucson, Arizona, 1978.
7. Risley, H.H., (1915), *The People of India,* W. Crooke, Calcutta.
8. Preamble of Constitution of India.
9. Chatterjee, S.K. (1945), *Language and the Linguistic Problem*, Oxford Phamplets on Indian affairs, No.II, London.
10. Karve, Irawati, *Kinship Organization in India,* Deccan College, Monography Series II, Poona, 1953, pp. 1-10.
11. Radhakrishna Dr. S. (1957), *The Hindu View of Life,* George Allen and Unwin, New York.
12. Dube, S. C. (1955), *Indian Village,* Cornell University Press, Ithaca.
13. Thirtha, N.V. (1960), "Rural Expectations Concerning Education in India" in *Teacher Education,* New Delhi, Nos. 7 & 8 July-Aug.
14. Ruhela, S.P. (1969), *Social Determinants of Educability in India,* Jain Brothers, New Delhi.
15. Shah, B.V. (1964), *Social Change in College Students of Gujarat,* M.S. University, Baroda.
16. Shrimali, K.L. (1970), *The Prospects for Democracy in India,* Southern Illinois University Press, USA.

3

Education: A Sub-System of Indian Society

Education is a process which helps in the achievement of the purposeful living the society and a society is a product of its social forces (caste, class, family etc.). In course of time its structure gets complex through process of social change. Education in this respect is a process which helps the members of the society to adopt the constantly changing aspect of society.

The society as a social system has its set goals which are attained through the process of integration and adaptation.

During the last few periods of educational history we have applied philosophical, psychological and technical approaches to the analysis of the process of education. Such approaches, it may be accepted, are not without yields (profit) but in our preoccupation with the philosophico-psycho-technological approaches we have perhaps underrated the existential social institutional forces which separate on the educational system. In such a state of our analysis there has emerged recently the sociological watershed which opens up new premises in our traditional interpretation of the perspectives of education in the moulding society.

1. One of the premises of sociology is that the individual is born into situations resulting from the operation of forces, historical and contemporary.
2. Education may be viewed as a self-contained social system

with a unique organisation and unique patterns. The second premise is that the individual in the process of his socialisation gets himself identified with the structure and goals of the society.

To the sociologist the concept of social system is useful in studying social structure and social organisation. A social system is a network or system of social interaction or more strictly a system of the actions of individuals—organised to carry out one or more essential tasks of a society.[1] According to Parsons and Shils: The principal unit of the system are roles and constellations of roles.

The educational system that we find today in our country stems from the Constitution and the historical character of educational aims in India—Education though a State subject is based on the collaboration of the Central government and the State government. Different Commissions and educational policies surveyed the entire field of educational development and make a comprehensive review of the country's educational system. The elementary education is the base of the system of education. If this level is well organised it has a far reaching influence on the upper levels of the system. The quality and size of this level substantially affects the higher secondary and the University education. The larger the base that is, the number of pupils in the 1 to 14-year-old group is school, the larger the possibilities of an increased number in secondary school and higher education.

Secondary education is run by the state governments, Central government, voluntary associations and missionary societies and public schools co-ordination in different schools is effected through Board of Secondary Education and the Central Board of Secondary Education. Theoretically, Indian Secondary Education suffers with the dilemma whether it should be a channel to higher education only or should be terminal education for the large masses of people. Secondary Education Commission (1952-53) observed that the Indian system of secondary education is entirely subservient to University education.

The purpose of University education in India was to create a class of people who would conform to the civilized norms of British society. University education has imparted specialised expert training. In the changing perspective the role of higher education is to aim at cultivating the students for a "conduct of life" and impart them specialised expert training. The universities in the country have their source of power and functions from various Acts of Central and State legislatures.[2] The Universities inter-system is run and maintained by Executive Council or Syndicates. The State Universities are financed by the State and Union Aid. The University Grants Commission provides grants for additional staff, library and Laboratory facilities, accommodation for teaching and research, books, furniture and equipment. UGC also advances special assistance to selected Universities departments to function as centres of Advanced Studies. These Centres aim at improving quality at the Post graduate and Research levels.

In the Indian context education today occupy a significant place in our national strategy which is directed towards the achievement of a democratic society which in its structure would be scientific, industrial-technological, but held up by the unit of linguistic regional sub-structure. They are structure units namely the states are required to identify themselves with the all India, societal structure of norms, values and goals.[3]

According to Clark:[4] Educational System has a definite bearing on the society which possesses it. The relation of economy, social stratification, culture and social integration is closely linked with education.

According to M.S. Gore and Others:[5] The Socialisation takes place with in the former system of education. Education system might primarily be looked upon as the agency for the transference and advancement of knowledge. Education is related to other aspects of social system, such as kinship, social stratification, political organisation and finally to knowledge and attitudes of knowledge, it also includes the organisational pattern of education; teacher pupil relationship, teacher administrator relationship, teacher relationship and student interaction.

Characteristics of Education Sub-System

The following are the characteristics of Education as a Social Sub-system:

1. Education is a strong agent towards building a social individualism. It develops norms, values, knowledge, understanding in an individual.
2. It helps to mould the society.
3. It studies the interaction system which emerges from the

structure and functioning of human groups and also helps the child to understand educational affairs.

4. Education system emerges as a result of the working of different institutions.
5. Like, other institution, educational institution provide opportunities for meeting man's need to pass on the desirable characteristics of his culture. It fulfils some human needs.
6. It is through the school system that the younger generation acquires the values and norms of the society. The school is the place where the transference of values and norms takes place.
7. Educational system involves an intricate (rigid) kind of control mechanism.
8. Educational system is a sub-system of the total system of the society.
9. Educational system sharpens the educational conceptualisation of tools and techniques enriches the discipline and gives new illumination towards the solution of educational problems.

Education and Its Relationship with Indian Social Structure

Inter-relationship between Education and Economy

With the advancement of industrialism when the economy shifts from agriculture to manufacturing and then the service industry, it very significantly affects the nature of educational institutions. Actually in such a situation the demands of society vary from manual to mental and from low to high degree of skills. In fact, with the advancing industrialism, the educational threshold of employment rises and there is a constant need for training persons in professional skills. In Indian situation education has become a prime need for developing our economy. Industrialisation emphasises research for pushing up more production perhaps at the level of sophisticated electronics. Higher education in research is the supplier of scientists and engineers for accelerating technological advance. In this situation some problems of sociological interest may also emerge wherein there may be lopsided development, in the sense that educational institutions over produce technicians and skilled persons thereby increasing unemployment. These are some of the basic approaches which characterise reciprocal relation between economy and education in a technological society.

In Indian society which is oriented to science and technology, education is considered more or less an industry and there are approaches to apply the concepts used in manufacturing industry for analysing the efficiency of education. Thus the modern trend of viewing education economically tempts social scientists to operationalise the concepts of rates of return, unit-costs and income-expenditure statement. The tools of industries such as profit and price mechanisms are also applied to analyse the problems of social benefits and social costs. When the country emphasises on science and technological education and higher research, much expenditure has to be incurred on education.[6] Expenditure on education incurred outlays on school building, hostels, library buildings, outlays on administration and other facilities, and purely educational outlays, like expenditure on teachers' salaries, scholarships, books and laboratory facilities. This seems to be a suitable postulate to assess the benefit cost and the rate of return in educational economy. To operationalise this industrial approach to education requires the construction of indices of efficiency of education. In absence of it our emphasis in this section would be to analyse the comprehensive links found in education and economic systems. In industrial society education is required to produce both new technology through research and professional and scientific manpower through training. This implies that the task of occupational and, therefore, social selection is increasingly centred on the school.

The modern school distributes life chances. Therefore, it is not surprising that educational opportunity becomes an object of wide political concern in industrial and industrialising countries. And the economic forces that demand higher educational standard also make possible the realisation of political aspirations that lead to a higher educational standard of living. These two forces together, underline the characteristic tendency in industrial countries towards expansion of educational systems.

B.V. Shah has given occupational background of the students in his study *"Social Change and College Students of Gujarat"* have observed that the students largely belong to the families which belong to higher status occupational groups.[7] His general conclusion is that nearly 52 per cent of the students come from families which are engaged in white collar occupations. Victor D'Souza in his study *"Education, Social Structure and Democracy in India"*, observed that the socio-economic background of the parents responsible for the quality of education of children."[8]

Economic structure as a determinant of educability clearly indicates that in the present set up of the society, despite the fact that there is equal opportunity for all, persons belonging to higher occupations or income groups get the benefit of a higher quality of education. If the trend indicates that economically advanced people get better educational opportunities, the logic leads us to say that the students coming out of better institutions would occupy higher occupational roles in the society, in the future Indian society the economic elites would continue to influence the decision-making at various levels.

Inter-relationship Between Education and Polity, Education and Politics

In ancient India there had been tradition of teachers and scholars exercising huge power on the rulers and the masses. Those who studied the *Vedas* and *Upnishadas* were given high status in the society. They acted as councillors and advisers to the rulers. Chanakya is well-known for his statecraftship. He dominated the total political scene of his times. In political paraphrase, the question as to who holds the power can hardly be answered satisfactorily in the absence of any valid date. But in the wake of the emerging nature and structure of elite and its democratisation, it appears that the economic elites have failed to gain a clearly preponderating influence upon decision-making. The creation of a socialist society has further discouraged the emergence of a bourgeoisie the economic elites who could influence substantially the process of decision-making. According to T.B. Bottomore, in the present India two elite groups—the high officials and the nationalist political leaders—have a predominant influence and are indeed responsible for the fortunes of India's effort to become a modern industrial nation. The function of education in the structure of power is significant for the social policy, and with the development. As a result of the educational facilities increasingly given to minority groups, a new class of men of power is also emerging. The new faces which appear in power structures are members of minorities, notably the Scheduled Tribes and the Scheduled Castes. The sources of power for these groups are Constitutional. They have been granted safeties and securities besides adequate facilities of education.

Among new men of power may also be included labour leaders. With the increase in factories and mills, the labourman power has increased and this has raised the status of labour leaders. They are experts in their field and this has secured them a position in the power structures.

The persons trained in schools and Universities and the gifted sons of the masses would in course of time claim a legitimate status to assimilation with the elite structure. When the country is passing through the process of modernisation, more and more services of technical, skilled and expert persons are required at the levels of decision-making and implementation.

Inter-relationship Between Education and Caste

The main aspects of Indian social stratification are the caste and the class systems. Caste may be defined as a "social class in which membership is determined by birth and from which there is virtually no vertical mobility," Castes are classified into the latter being a category granted some constitutional safeguards and securities. These constitutional efforts provide equal opportunities to Backward Castes and other classes. Special facilities in education in this respect are given to these sections. The class categories are in our country dominant social determinants of educability.

In the study of B.V. Shah referred to above, very few students come from the lower castes. "Out of 200 students, 38 per cent are Banias, 26 are Balidars, and 24 are Brahmins. Thus only 3 upper castes account for 88 per cent of students."[10] Of course it should be admitted that the lower castes were reluctant during the previous decades in sending their children even to the high schools. Today they have come forward for elementary schooling but the fact remains that very few students of lower castes come to the higher educational institutions. B.V. Shah informs that the lower castes constitute 91.5 per cent of the total number of 200 students whereas the higher education has remained a main preserve of the upper castes.

Again to quote the study of Victor D'Souza, among the Hindu castes such as artisans and allied castes, the status of education is better than the category of warrior and trading. This is accounted for the urban industrial setting of Dandeli which provides facilities to the artisan caste to acquire skilled occupation relatively more easily and improve their educational background. Concluding his findings D'souza says that "the caste and occupational background of parents influence the education of children as regards the degree of illiteracy, the amount of education and the quality of education."[11]

Inter-relationship Between Education and Religion

In an ancient society such as our own the social functions of religion have greater significance in regard to the development of education. Religion of India besides emphasising on *moksha* or *salvation*, also motivates a person to better his life on earth. During the ancient times religion in India was a dominant social determinant of educability. For instance, the untouchables and the lower caste people were denied at the outset the chances of getting any education. On the other hand it was obligatory for a Brahmin to read the *vedas* and acquire all the classical knowledge. With the passage of time this determinating role of religion gradually weakened. Nevertheless, religion even today is to some extent significant determinant of educability though on surface level it may appear that religion has lost its influence with reference to the growing impact of science and technology. Today the structure of religion has become more complex. First, though most religious sects specify their formal set of beliefs, not all adherents of the sect subscribe in equal measure to all of the formal doctrine. Second, there are a large number of people who do not regularly or occasionally go to worship the deity at a shrine, but still claim some adherence to a given religious denomination. Third, an individual's religious beliefs are not static but are subject to change. "Some of the greatest changes in belief occur during adolescence, a period of life which frequently seizes youths' religious ideas more from a childlike acceptance or orthodoxy to a definition of new connections. The emerging critically examined beliefs tend to deviate from the traditional doctrine of their particular denomination."[12]

In our country religion constitutues an area of life where the State does not interfere. This has rendered Indian society a multi-religious society. Hindu, Buddhist, Jain, Sikh, Parsi, Christian and

Muslims constitute the Indian social structure as adherents of various religions.

Both Hinduism and Islam even today discourage education to women theoretically. The Hindu women have largely taken to education but there are still some inhibitions among some Muslim women to take to education and more specially University one. The other religions do not exhibit any distinct opposition for giving education to females.

We do not have any scientifically collected data on the bearing of education on educability except that Victor D'souza refers to the three major religious categories of Hindus, Muslims and Christians inhibiting the industrial community of Dandeli, referred to earlier. Dandeli consisted of migrants and their progeny who have immigrated during the past 40 years or so. Percentage distribution of adults over 14 years of age by population groupings and status of education indicate that among Hindus the percentage of illiterate is lesser than the Muslims and the Christians. Similarly, at the higher standard of education Hindus score over the Muslims and the Christians. D'souza while informing about the school age children (6-13) states that among Hindus the Brahmins have a percentage of 96.8 of school going children. This comes to 88.4 per cent of Karwar Muslims and 81.7 for Kanara Christians. Negatively, the percentage of children who stopped going to school comes to 1.6 among Hindus which rises to 4.9 and 8.7 for Kanwar Muslims and other Muslims respectively. The study of D'souza provides data which reveal that Hinduism is more prone to educability.

Caste and Education

The main aspects of Indian social stratification are the caste and the class systems. Caste may be defined as a "social class in which Membership is determined by birth and from which there is virtually no vertical mobility."[13] Caste are classified into the latter being a category granted some constitutional safeguards and securities. These constitutional efforts provide equal opportunities to Backward Castes and classes. Special facilities in education in this respect are given to these sections. The class categories are in our country dominant social determinants of educability.

In the study of B.V. Shah referred to above, very few students come from the lower castes. "Out of 200 students, 38 per cent are Banias, 26 are Balidars, and 24 are Brahmins. Thus only 3 upper castes account for 88 per cent of students."[14] Of course it should be admitted that the lower castes were reluctant during the previous decades in sending their children even to the high schools. Today they have come forward for elementary schooling but the fact remains that very few students of lower castes come to the higher educational institutions. B.V. Shah informs that the lower castes constitute 91.5 per cent of the total number of 200 students whereas the higher education has remained a main preserve of the upper castes.

Again to quote the study of Victor D'souza, among the Hindu castes such as artisans and allied castes, the amount of education is better than the category of warrior and trading. This is accounted for the urban industrial setting of Dandeli which provides facilities to the artisan caste to acquire skilled occupation relatively more easily and improve their educational background. Concluding his findings D'souza says that "the caste and occupational background of parents influences the education of children as regards the degree of illiteracy, the amount of education and the quality of education."[15]

Inter-Relationship Between Education and Culture

In an industrial society education is faced with two crises—accessibility and adequacy of education. Adequacy will continue to grow as a problem in view of cultural and social changes and accessibility to higher education would increase with the increasing complexity of the society. Education is closely linked up with the social system in the sense that the former maintains cultural continuity and at the same time works for cultural change. Cultural change is a change in the basic structure, function or interrelationship in a social system such as a group, a social institution or a society. Education is a dominant factor for cultural and social change. On the one hand, education has to maintain the core values and on the other to introduce the values of secularism and rationality in the Indian Society. The prime aim of Social change in any society is to achieve progress. The school and the university modify the ideas and concepts of progress in the mental constructs of the students. The school and the university, therefore, are involved in the problem of conservation, experimentation, reconstruction of the alternatives available in the society.[16] The educational institutions in fact operationalise the norms, values and goals desired by social change. The school is a battle ground where traditionalism and modernity confront each other. The class room reflects the change that would come in the society. In Indian culture there are three major sub-structures:

1. Elite,
2. Folk,
3. Tribal

The elites want change in democratic principles. The folk and tribal strata of Indian Society are experiencing a kind of social mobility by getting education. For the first time a new mode of interaction between the sub-cultures has emerged. Education is a strong factor in widening the gulf between the elites and the masses.

Education as an Instrument for Social Change

A society wishing to change or modernise itself has to employ or use a number of means, instruments, institutions, agents or agencies to achieve its desired goals. Among such means, education is perhaps the most important or at least one of the most important ones. It is hopefully believed by most people that education will provide necessary training in skills and accupations and thus produce the needed competent personnel for manning the different specialised jobs in modern industrial, business, educational and research establishments and secondary associations. Not only this, education is expected to change the values and attitudes of people and to create in them an urge or the necessary motivation to achieve social class ascendency, social mobility and/or their sanskritisation. It is now widely held that modern education can mould people into enlightened, empathetic, risk-taking, thick-skinned, industrious and mobile personalities. That education will be of an immense help in bringing about democratisation, secularism, national integration as well as economic prosperity and proper political socialisation in the given country is yet another great expectations of leaders. It is generally believed by people that axe of education can cut down the thick roots of traditions, superstitions, ignorance, backwardness, parchialism etc. The timid owls of conventional stupidity or illogicality will fly away as soon as the sunlight of education falls on the particular society. The minds of even a very dull, pessimistic and traditionally unmotivated people can be stirred up by the instrumentality of modern education. Education can help people in knowing their weaknesses or gaps of knowledge, and in enabling them to gain necessary knowledge in order to achieve progress in all spheres of their life in a systematic or consistent manner.

These pious belief's, assumptions or expectations about the role of education in bringing about social change and modernisation (in fact modernisation is also a kind of change) have led leaders, planners as well as developing nations to make huge provisions of educational facilities for their respective people. We in India have also seen the great efforts of our educational planners during the last fifteen or sixteen years of national planning to expand diverse sorts of educational facilities at all levels, and in all regions of the country. In a bid to leapfrog to modernisation, we have not hesitated to tame "white elephants" like th I.I.Ts, (Indian Institutes of Technololgy), R.C.Es (Regional Colleges of Education), and the national laboratories. Like many of the developing nations, India has also readily accepted all sorts of loans and gifts from the prosperous nations irrespective of their economic ideologies. Foreign educational experts have been pouring in here to train or educate our personnel and students, and our scholars and teachers have also been going out to receive higher education or training in the foreign universities and institutions of advanced learning. Eager to modernise ourselves as early as possible, we have been and are still very prompt in borrowing and experimenting with all sorts of new ideas, theories, practices and mechanisms in almost all aspects of our national education, no matter at whatever cost and with what ultimate results. They have resulted in many good things although much change still remains to be brought about.

It is interesting to note here how even some mutually opposite things have been emphasised in India in the name of this role of education. Thus, for example, while both Maulana A. K. Azad[17] and Dr. K. L. Shrimali[18] had emphasised that they were making all out efforts to popularise Basic education in order to bring about social change in the country, we have seen how during the tenure of their three successors Basic Education has been dethroned just in order to bring about social change and modernisation in India.

We have so far viewed the second form of relationship between education and social change from the point of view of the society.

But if we go further and try to analyse the lives of individual citizens in India, we shall find two interesting changes coming up:

Firstly, more and more people of the lower and middle classes (and especially the lower and lower middle classes) are now making great sacrifices so that their children may get educated now and with their education they may be able to make their living satisfactorily;

Secondly, more and more people of the lower castes are now becoming successful in sanskritising themselves by dint of their higher education, migration to towns and cities and hiding themselves in the crowds of anonymity and unconcern for each other and secularism. Education has certainly enabled them in changing their lives for the better; it has granted them better social status and opened the flood-gates of aspirations for their children.

Education must emphasise social reform with the similar spirit, perspective and force as social reform movements like Brahmo Samaj, Arya Samaj, Protestantism etc. showed. Mere liberalism and openness to western or modern influences is not sufficient. Concrete programmes of social action warranted by the contemporary Indian society, which could not be taken up during the last twenty years of freedom, must now be seriously accomplished within the shortest possible time through the proper use of education as the means. Without a renovated programme of adult or social education it cannot be done. Similarly, without making education a multipurpose tool, the desired social changes cannot come up. Our curricula must really change and become modern.

Our teachers should and can certainly help the nation in bringing about long awaited social changes. They have, themselves, first of all, to become mabile personalities with high degree of empathy, achievement, motivation, social sensitivity, risk taking capability and similar other attributes of a modern man. It is only than that they can activate or generate the minds and energies of our youth. How many teachers even college teachers, have any vision or picture of modernity in India in the next fifteen or twenty years in their minds? Are they preparing their students for taking their right places in such a future society? So long as they do not understand this and involve themselves whole-heartedly in generating the process of social change in India, they will remain alienated from the other sections of our changing society and will be blamed by the future generations for inaction and deceit. Several sociological studies like those of Shils, Cormack, Shah, Ruhela etc. have shown that today even most of our University students are more or less traditional in their values and they do not have enough courage to accept and hold for long modern values. When they are such, it can well be imagined what the plight of our school students and non-school youth would be. All categories of teachers in India have this as a very great challenge before them.

We are conscious of the fact that merely teachers cannot do all this unless their reference groups—the educational planners, educational administrators, political and social leaders and parents also come to the help of the teachers by modernising their working in their own spheres of social action. A study of the election manifestos of our political parties with a view to analyse what the latter have to say about education in India done by S.P. Ruhela[19] shows that our politicians have not given a proper place to education in their schemes of things. The educational programmes suggested by the rightist parties like the Congress, Swatantra, BJP and Hindu Mahasabha are fewer and much lesser in dynamism and modernism than those suggested by the leftist parties— both the communist parties which are eager to use violent methods for bringing about social change in the country with the help of teachers, students, intellectuals and also army as and when possible. There is need for all parties to discuss amongst themselves the educational needs of the country and arrive at a consensus on a core programme of education to be implemented in the country inspite of their varied political moorings. The educational bureaucracy, still dominated by many old stereotyped immobile personalities in Ministries, Universities, directorates, colleges and schools, must also change. The parents, who are also suffering from the inaction and tyranny of change, must change and instead of remaining in apathy towards what goes on in schools and colleges, they must take greater initiative and interest in aiding education in changing our society. In the final analysis, the ultimate responsibility of activating all these reference groups and enlisting their functional support in the great task of changing and modernising our society through education would fall on the shoulders of teachers. The sooner they realise it the better.

Social Demand for Education

There is every reason to believe that the social demand for a longer education will continue to increase. We have noted the trend to stay in full-time education until the ages of seventeen or eighteen, and hence become potential candidates for higher education, and we have given evidence to show that we are still losing boys and girls of good ability in their struggle throughout complex and class-stratified educational system. A greater appreciation of the value of a longer education is spreading throughout all levels of society. This is specially noticeable among working-class parents who are more than ever before willing, and even anxious, to let their children stay on beyond the statutory leaving age. The pressure on our system to respond and adapt to the demand is being felt in three major directions which will now be considered.

(a) The Universities and Higher Education

The modern university not only continues its traditional functions as a community of scholars and a centre for the advancement of knowledge and research, but has also become a source of recruitment for the leading positions of power and influence in society. With the continuing and large increase in the professional and managerial classes the universities come to have more and more sociological significance. They are finding themselves more closely linked with specialised occupational interest, and are called upon to examine their place and change the direction of their influence in a world becoming more geared to material production. In fact, alongwith the newer institutions of higher learning, they are now becoming a crucial factor in the development of our national economy. This is a great change from the traditional functions of a university. Until well into this century the ancient universities were able to remain relatively aloof from the economic problems of the society. Originally part of the religious rather than the economic life they became, with the secularisation of knowledge, agencies for transmitting a traditional culture and conserving the status of certain elites.

We must face the possibility of many more willing and able students coming forward than the capacity of our higher educational institutions is at present planned to deal with. What has been said about the universities equally applies to the colleges of advanced technology, and the teachers' training colleges. If provision is made for training, and strictly on this condition, it means that there need not be any serious concern about finding the necessary number of scientists and technologists for the next stage of expansion which the Government thinks the economy needs. There will also be enough to expand the supply of teachers. But when these targets are reached do we again limit our output of specialists to that particular elite. Will our 18 plus selection mean the rejection of many who would be capable of a higher education? This raises the question of whether our educational system should be so closely tied to occupational needs. It is desirable for each individual to have the education which best suits his capacities, whatever his later work in life turns out to be. The development of such a genuinely educative society calls for the continuous adaptation of our educational institutions to meet the needs of its members.

(b) More Secondary Education

There is a demand for a longer school life in schools. There is already a voluntary raising of the school-leaving age, and hence the increase of extended courses. According to the Crowther Report in the end would not be enough, and they make a strong case for raising the school-leaving age to sixteen. There are one or two things which should be said about this from a sociological point of view.

With the raising of the school leaving age it is unlikely that more than half, at most, of the pupils would be prepared for an external examination for sometime to come. Among the rest are two groups of pupils which would cause particular concern. The first consists of the backward and immature boys and girls, who may be physically as well as mentally below average. The Report stages there is probably a larger group, who are physically quite as well developed as any boys or girls of their age, and who are straining at the least to get out into the world.' These are later referred to as 'these reluctant pupils', and many of them contribute to the juvenile delinquency rate which reaches its peak in the last year at school, and is reduced during the first year at work. Many of them would also be among the one-fifth of the boys and one-quarter of the girls who, in the Social Survey, gave as the main reason why they left at the earliest possible moment, the plain fact that they disliked school. If these two groups of pupils are to be kept at school for a further year it is certain that the schools must be prepared to extend their function of providing a protective, moral and even therapeutic environment for the adolescent. Much is already being done for the backward and immature, and a greater provision of suitable courses and teachers for them is urgent. But for an added responsibility to be successfully undertaken for the tougher group we need some assurance that we can get more of the right sort of teachers who can deal with, and interest, these 'reluctant pupils', for whom the school is not at present a sufficiently attractive place. It must be recognised that we face a teenage problem, the resolution of which depends very much on establishing the right relationships between adults and adolescents. It is thus a matter of extreme importance that the ordinary school should become a community which is congenial, helpful and useful in developing young people, no longer children, who are passing through what, in our society, is a difficult period of growth. Therefore we must feel as sure as possible that the necessary changes in provision will be ready before compelling this unwilling section of youth to remain at school. Otherwise they will be under conditions which might harden their resentment, and increase their sense of rebellion against a society which appears not to understand them, and has failed to enlist their loyalty or co-operation. No doubt this change in the nature and social climate of schools can happen, in time, and they will become places where the pupils will want to stay. This would be the best way to raise the school-leaving age.

The chief argument in the national interest for the compulsory raising of the school-leaving age is the wastage of talent.

(c) Technical Education

The demand for technical education has been increasing rapidly. We refer here to the training of top and middle-grade technicians below the level of the technologists. These have, in the past, mostly been educated by part-time courses in which there has been a shortage of time, a heavy failure rate, and lack of breadth. There has also been a need for a closer integration between schools and the system of further education. For example there has often been a gap of one year between leaving school and entering a Technical College.

The part-time basis of all courses has always been a difficulty, and arrangements are being made to give more time to a day-release scheme, often in the form of continuous periods known as 'block release'. Ultimately the development of sandwich courses for the sixteen to eighteen age range will be a still more satisfactory method, particularly if they are 'college based', which means that students are paid for by the local education authority while at college, and paid by their employers while at work. Forging a closer link between the schools and technical education is the most important aspect of these reforms, which come directly as a result of the failure of the system to keep pace with the changing needs of industry. The Technical College is just as the sixth form works towards the university. The provision of a ladder through all the various grades of technical courses also provide a route for the boy of ability, even if he leaves school early, which can lead to the highest qualifications in this field. It is likely that this alternative road through a creative and practical education in highly skilled work will become a major highway of the future, leading to satisfying, well-regarded and important positions in the occupational structure.

A school carries on an organised life of its own as a social group within the wider society around it. It is a community in the sense in which the majority of its members are children who are not yet ready to be full members of society, and are at school partly for this very purpose of becoming socialised.

The Spens Report of England refers to the school as 'a social unit or society of a peculiar kind'. The full passage reads as follows.... a typical school of the present day is to be regarded as not merely a 'place of learning' but as a social unit or society of a peculiar kind in which the older and younger members, the teachers and the taught, share a common life, subject to a constitution to which all are in their several ways consenting and co-operating parties. This passage suggests that the school itself should have a social structure on the democratic model as the use of the words 'consenting and co-operating parties' would imply. The Report in fact devotes several sections to describing practical methods for the training of boys and girls for life in a free community by an education which 'encourages initiative and the shouldering of responsibility from the earliest years'. This part of the Report is entitled 'The School as a Society' and makes the following definite suggestions which are summarised breifly as:

(i) That pupils themsevels should take some share in making the school rules.

(ii) That a greater number of pupils, not only the prefects, should take a share in responsibility.

(iii) *(a)* That it is wrong for the staff to control too much, especially societies and clubs outside the class room.

(b) That more minor organisation should be left to the pupils, even if done more easily by the staff—indeed that more opportunity should be given to the pupils to learn through making their own mistakes.

(iv) That there should be closer relations between the school and the adult society outside.

This matter is also referred to in a more recent official publication which is the pamphlet 'Citizens Growing Up'. There is a section on 'The School as a Community', in which the question is raised of how far a school can be organised on a democratic basis. If the school is to be concerned with practical citizenship it must obviously be preparing active members for the kind of society in which the pupils will ultimately play their part.

There is a point of view which insists that the imitation by the school community of the outside society can be carried too far. Children are immature and dependent, and it is not possible nor proper, it is said, for them to attempt to frame the rules governing their own life. They have their own social life and it is enough preparation for the future that this should be healthy one. In answer to this it would be granted that any complete form of self-government on the model of political democracy is impracticable, since it would involve electing their own teachers. What is required is a gradual process. In order to train the young in the ways of the adult society they should gradually be given more and more independence; they should experience more freedom and responsibility as they grow up. As John Dewey said: 'The only way to prepare for social life is to engage in social life.' A person cannot suddenly become a free adult. If it be granted that children are part of the non-social community this is not a reason for keeping them all the time under authoritarian rule. The continuous use of force towards children is not the best way to train them to treat others with kindness and respect.

Democracy in School Life

What can in practice be done in the school? The essence of democratic control is the sharing of power and influence by methods of delegation and consultation. It is possible to distinguish various areas of control which can be shared in different degrees between the staff and the pupils.

(i) Staff Control

General educational policy is clearly a matter for the staff, and the headmaster or headmistress will have the final word as representing the governors of the school or the local authority. Some of the rules will need to be made by the staff alone without any discussion with the pupils. Most punishment should be in the hands of the staff. Curriculum and teaching method are usually solely under staff control, but here certain forms of consultation and discussion with the pupils are possible.

(ii) Consultation with the Pupils

Consultation over curriculum can take place when there is a choice of courses, and the pupils' wishes can be considered. This becomes more and more possible in school work when a form of Dalton Plan or other individual assignment method is used, or as project methods are developed. Over rules and school organisation there are systems whereby an advisory body of pupils asked to make suggestions to the Head or to the Staff Meeting Alternatively a representative group of pupils may be consulted in advance over changes the Head wishes to make. School Councils which are purely advisory and have no executive powers would come under this heading.

(iii) Committees of Equal Co-operation

This name is given to all committees where staff and pupils meet, and under a certain constitution meet as equals for the purpose in hand. Ordinary examples are house meetings, form meetings, etc. especially when concerned with the election of officers and their own internal business. This is the place where those school councils would fit where staff and pupils are both represented. There may also be special committees for such things as the school magazine, the library, or for entertainments, where staff and pupils co-operate on equal terms. The essence of this type of council or committee is that decisions can be made within certain defined limits, and these can only be reversed by a special veto of the Head which might never in fact be used.

(iv) Pupil Control

This does not mean absolute control, but that the decisions of the pupils have the dominant influence, and in most cases are not challenged. The Prefect system is an example of pupil control, which is, however, really a form of delegated authority. Prefects will usually have some powers of punishment, and a certain sphere of control within which they can make their own decisions. The organisation of school games, and the various out-of-school societies and clubs can be left almost entirely to the pupils, although this is often not done. Members of staff can of course be closely associated with these activities, but not in a position of control. With regard to school work there are certain projects and free choice periods where initiative can be invited from the pupils with the minimum of staff interference. This likewise applies to hobbies which are sometimes conducted in school hours.

Shared Responsibility

Another feature of a democratic school community is that responsibility is learnt, in appropriate ways, by the younger as well as the older pupils. At all stages, and in work as well as in play, school children can be allowed a much fuller participation in the choice and organisation of what they are doing than was possible in the schools of past, where a more rigid control was the accepted method of teaching. Responsibility grows from having a definite role to play in the group. It is through the role plays and the child's feeling of significance in the group grows, and if he does not feel significant he cannot feel responsible. It can only be learnt by practice. If the child starts by being given a task well within his powers he can then make progress by gradually taking on more difficult responsibilities.[20]

Many schools plan a system of duties whereby as many pupils as possible, from the lowest forms upwards have some duty to perform for the whole community or some section of it is wider than just their own form or class group. It is a common enough practice to give class-room duties and these should be regularly changed and kept alive by criticism and discussion at class meetings. The carrying out of a duty for the larger group is worth the trouble it takes in organising, and the ingenuity required to think out the largest possible number of significant duties in a graded order of difficulty. The responsibility for people is the highest of all, and is given in the most obvious way to the sub-prefects and prefects.

The training for leadership and initiative can be extended into other fields outside the conventional ones of games and community discipline. In England the most useful opportunity for this is a fuller development of societies and clubs run by the pupils themselves. The children in a school need time that they can devote entirely to their own ends, and which allows them the maximum of self-activity not under the control or direct suggestion of an adult. This time will usually have to be taken from out-of-class hours, but some schools manage to arrange for societies and hobby clubs, etc., to meet for part of the time at least in school hours and then continue after school. Given the opportunity it is surprising how the junior as well as the senior groups will organise themselves and how leaders emerge. The seriousness with which children engage in these activities, and the hard work they sometimes carry out on things which interest them can also be observed when more individual freedom is given in ordinary classes which, far from being a waste of time, gives rise to really self-directed work. This is one of the basic assumptions of modern teaching method. The whole distinction (in terms of the children's feelings) between work and play tends to disappear when children find out that they can do just as important things on their own initiative as under the control of the teacher.

It can be seen that those so-called 'activity' methods which involve co-operation in groups have also an important influence on the social life of the school. Learning to work together, which in the old days would have been called 'cheating' or 'cribbing' has now become a virtue. This is an indication that changes are on the way in our culture, which is still largely individualistic and competitive. Team work has been praised and encouraged in games and in war, with remarkable success, but the spirit of the team in everyday workrelations is only just beginning to be appreciated. There are many task where the feelings of belonging to a group and working together with others for a common purpose adds energy and incentive to the participants.

The co-operation of groups depends on free discussion, which is another aspect of the democratic process. Discussion methods could be used much more at all levels in the school community, for instance between staff and staff as well as between staff and pupils, and between pupil groups under their own leadership.

Discussion can sometimes achieve better communication of ideas, and more often better relations between people by the communication of feelings and decisions within the group. The group situation is basic to the school programme whether it be the class, the practical work group, the school club, the team, the prefects' meeting, the school council or the staff meeting.

The organisation of the school community, the sharing of responsibility, the teaching methods, and the co-operation of groups all depend on the personal relations between people, the attitudes towards discipline and the use of authority.

The Social Climate of the School

People's relations within a social group create a kind of atmosphere which can be called the 'social climate'. A group may be felt to be a happy or an unhappy one. That is the impression it gives to strangers. The word 'morale' can be used, and there is a certain feeling when morale is good or poor. The problem is to study what lies behind the social climate of a school community, and try to discover some of the factors which go to make a happy school with high morale, and those which lead to failure to achieve good morale and cause unhappy social relationships.

Sharing a common life in a school implies certain kinds of relations, human relations, between people in a small community. Once we grant that part of a school's function is to prepare for social living the nature of these human relations becomes of critical importance. This is not the whole of education for citizenship but it is the vital part of it which is often neglected. Social living is not concerned so much with text-book facts as with behaviour.

What seems so extraordinary is the high degree of acceptance both in official and unofficial quarters of the importance of democratic social relations in the school, compared with the remarkably few practical measures that have actually been tried in the schools to bring about this state of affairs.

The Use of Authority

We have so far assumed that we have called democratic social relations are the most desirable in our schools. It must be pointed out that this is nevertheless an assumption, but it is justified if we accept the social philosophy on which our concept of the democratic society is based, and if in fact the methods employed lead to the behaviour we desire. The practical test is to obtain some objective evidence of the kind of behaviour which results from the methods we call democratic, compared with the methods we call authoritarian, or any other methods we choose to observe. We should still have to make the value judgement on which results we considered more desirable, but the first step is scientific and involves recording and classifying the behaviour under different conditions.

In England this work was carried out with selected groups of boys in youth clubs, where the leaders artificially created different atmospheres which were classified as authoritarian, democratic, or laissez-faire. For details of the experimental methods of these lengthy studies reference must be made to the original papers. A few of the results with implications for the school situation can be summarised as follows. The autocratic leader determined the work to be done, and dictated the stages of work step by step. He decided each boy's task and with whom he should work. He gave orders, or disruptive commands, or non-constructive criticism, or showed other behaviour of this checking kind twelve times as much as the democratic leader. The democratic leader allowed the work to be determined wherever possible by group discussion. He gave encouragement and practical advice, and the further stages of the work were foreseen by the group right from the beginning.

Domination with Evidence of Conflict

Conflict is defined as working against the wish of the child, who shows his intention do not correspond with the teacher's and he usually resists or objects. For example the teacher may order the child's activity, in conflict with him, by such familiar remarks as 'Sit still Don't do that put those things away how many times have I told you not to...' All direct refusal, disapproval, blame or shame, warnings, threats and punishments especially when no reason or explanation is given by the teacher which is acceptable to the child, come into this category.

Dominatin with Evidence of Working Together

Working together is defined as the teacher and the child pursuing the same goal with a common purpose, and without imposition by the teacher. Acceptance under pressure from the teacher is not working together. When there is an element of domination remaining, the teacher always decides, but the child's wishes are considered. That the teacher selects activity for the child on the basis of his interest is typical of this form of working together, but the teacher still plans all the work.

Integration with Evidence of Working Together

Here co-operation is based on the child's expressed initiative, and he is allowed to contribute freely his suggestions and wishes. The child is accepted as a partner in the enterprise, which he often shows that he wanted. Inspite of being 'wrong' the child's views are attended to, examined and tested. The teacher will help the child advance and solve his own problem, and gives approval and agreement to the spontaneous and self-initiated behaviour of the child, following whenever possible the child's expressed wish, suggestion or need.

Anderson and Brewer also worked out categories of child response to the attitudes and actions of the teachers. Thus during any period of observation in a classroom a check was made of each item of behaviour on the part of the teacher, and each item on the part of any child in the room.

The Roles of the Teacher

The teacher, like any other member of society, plays many social roles in accordance with the different statuses he occupies both in his private and public life. But the nature of the teacher's occupation places him in the special position of having a complicated set of roles in connection with his occupation alone. He is, as it were, in between the world of youth and the adult world, trying to meet the claims of his pupils while reconciling them with the expectations of their parents, and relating both to the needs of society at large. He has on the one hand an academic role concerned with scholarship, and on the other hand, he is a character-trained, concerned with the development of the child's whole personality. The teacher's principal roles can be listed briefly as follows:

(i) The Teacher as an Academic Specialist

This is the teacher's traditional role. He is expected to know his subject, and to be the acknowledged superior to his pupils in this respect. Nevertheless he must be prepared to face the fact that some of his pupils will be potentially, or actually, clever than he is, and any teacher should be willing to admit when he makes a mistake. There is a type of teacher who values very highly his standard of scholarship, and another type who sees himself in the role of an all-round educator. Each has his place in a school. At the same time one hopes that the specialists will avoid the charge of narrowness, and will see the point of growing trend towards a broader education at school age.

(ii) The Teacher as a Methodologist

The teacher is also expected to be an expert in the methods of teaching and learning. He may exercise this role in different ways, and all that has been said in this chapter on the dominative and integrative attitudes of teachers is very relevant here. In watching a teacher in the classroom the observer will notice how far he encourages passive or active learning, how far the lesson is teacher-centred or pupil-centred, how much it is a lecture and how much a discussion.

There are different social conditions for successful learning, according to the nature and stage of the learning process. Learning in class takes place in a group situation. The teacher's general task is to establish that learning is the expected behaviour in the classroom, and is the principal goal of the group.

The learning situations produce a different social climate in the classroom from those, also necessary at other times, in which the teacher stands in front of the class, does most of the talking, and uses a rapid question-and-answer technique. The choice of method is within the power of the teacher, and he should always be aware that in making his choice he is determining the nature of a social situation. His general objective is obtaining a relationship between the class and the task which is before them.

(iii) The Teacher as a Character-trainer

To be able to keep good discipline is a highly valued quality in a teacher. There are different methods of achieving this end, covering a range of sanctions from enforcing a strict code of punishment to the gentle but effective persuasion by personal influence. There is, of course, more in discipline than keeping order, and the objective is the development of a capacity for self-discipline. This brings out the function of a teacher as a counsellor or advisor. If the pupil is lacking an interest or unwilling to make the effort to learn, the first concern of the teacher is to find the reason, and then to remove the obstacle to learning. Anti-social conduct must also have its cause, and the teacher will try to understand the pupil's motivation, and act with the intention of seeking a cure rather than imposing a standard punishment.

(iv) The Teacher as a Member of a School Staff

He is a member of the teaching hierarchy both in his school, and in the general educational system. Each school has a formal structure of authority, from the headmaster downwards through varying degrees of seniority. The new assistant, who is also a beginner, will have to learn the role which is expected of him in his new situation. The formal structure is not necessarily rigid, and the case of social relations between teachers of different seniority varies very much from school to school.

(v) The Teacher as a Member of Society

The teacher will himself be a member of a particular sub-culture within society. He will have acquired certain standards of behaviour from his upbringing which will influence his classroom and staff-room relationships. There has in the past been some uncertainty over the social class of teachers.

Whatever his personal views may be, the fact stands out that the teacher has a role as a representative of adult society. This is the ultimate source of his authority. He is responsible for the socialisation of the young on behalf of the adult society for which they are being prepared. The way he uses his authority may vary, but whatever he does he cannot abdicate, and must accept his responsibilities. The pupils will react to him, as they will to all authority figures, in different ways, but while they are in his care it is his duty to be the moralist and the final arbiter of the rules.

References

1. Bhattacharya and Sriniwas (1977), *Society and Education*, Academic Pub., Calcutta.
2. Charlos, P. Loomis (1960), *Social System: Essays on their Persistence Changes VI*, Van Nostrand Co.
3. Chitnis, Suma (1974), *Sociology of Education in a Survey of Research in Sociology and Social Anthropology*, Vol. II, I.C.S.S.R., New Delhi.

4. Clark, Burton R., "Sociology of Education", Rand Mcnally and Co. Chicago.
5. Gore, M.S. and Others (1967), *Papers in the Sociology of Education in India,* NCERT, New Delhi.
6. Durkhiem, Emile (1956), "Education and Sociology," *The Free Press,* New York.
7. Shah, B.V. (1964), *Social Change and College Students of Gujarat,* M.S. University, Baroda.
8. D'Souza, Victor, "Education, Social Structure and Democracy in India", Ph.D. thesis, M.S. University, Baroda.
9. Bottomore, T.B., *Education and Society.*
10. B. V. Shah, *Ibid.*
11. D'Souza, Victor, *Ibid.*
12. John. D.V. (1937), 'Education and Social Change', *Social Frontier,* 3rd May.
13. Ottawa Y., A.K.C. (1962), *Education and Society,* Routeledge & Kegan Paul.
14. B.V. Shah, *Ibid.*
15. D'Souza, Victor, *Ibid.*
16. Persons, Talcott (1951), Social System, *Free Press,* U.S.A.
17. Azad, A.K., *Basic Education.*
18. Shrimali, K.L., *Basic Education.*
19. Ruhela, S.P., *Sociological Basis of Education.*
20. Tayler, William (1977), *The Sociology of Educational Inequality,* Methuen & Co. Ltd.

4

Education as a Process in the Social System: A Social Activity

A society is a product of its own social forces. In course of time its structure gets complexity through process of social change. Education in this respect is a process which helps the members of society to adopt to the constantly changing aspect of society. The society as a social system has its set goals which are attained through the process of integration and adapation.[1]

During the last few periods of educational history we have applied philosophical, psychological and technical approaches to the analysis of the process of education. Such approaches it may be accepted are not without yields (profit). But in our preoccupation with the philosophico-psycho-technological approaches we have perhaps underrated the existential social institutional forces which operate on the educational system. In such a state of our analysis there has emerged recently the sociological watershed which opens up new premises in our traditional interpretation of the perspectives of education in the moulding of society:

1. One of the premises of sociology is that the individual is born into situations resulting from the operation of forces historical and contemporary.
2. The second premise is that the individual in the process of his socialisation gets himself identified with the structure and goals of the society.

Education may be viewed as a self-contained social system with a unique organisation and unique patterns of expectations for its members.

What is Social System ?

To the sociologist the concept of social system is useful in studying social structure and social organization. A social system is a network or system of social interactions—or more strictly a system of the actions of individuals—organized to carry out one or more essential tasks of society (Robert J. Havighurst and Bernice L. Neugarten, p. 269).[2]

According to persons and shils the principal units of the system are roles and constellations of roles.[3]

Education as a Process in the Social System

The educational system is one among many social systems such as local government business organizations, social welfare agencies and churches. It is a set of roles and constellations which has been devised for the purpose of systematically teaching children and adults a variety of information, skills and attitudes that people are not likely to learn efficiently in the family or in work situations[4] for example a police system is a set of roles and roles constellations designed to protect order and to enforce the law.

Role Analysis of Education as a Social System

School system operates by its sub-systems. Teachers carry out their teaching responsibilities. Pupils, Principal Superintendent, School board all in terms in the way in which their roles are performed. Different studies would provide a picture of how the school operates as a social system and how the system maintains itself, even though different individuals move in and out of particular roles.[5] One may study the ineractions between social systems in terms of role analysis, i.e., principal or the Superintendent or the teachers general relate in other institutional representatives or so on. Any social system relates to any other by the interactions of the people who fill the roles in the two systems.

Relations among Educational Sub-Systems

The educational sub-system consist of the various institutions or schools i.e., public school districts in the area: the system of Roman Catholic schools, the system of Lutheran schools, other church related school systems such as the Christian schools and the seventh day Adventist schools and the independent private schools.

These sub-systems have had a tradition of working separately. But there is some cooperation between different nature of schools.

Relations Between Educational and Other Social System

In order to study relationship between educational and other social systems, the social systems can be divided into two categories—[6]

1. Critical, and
2. Supporting systems.

A supporting system is one which performs its functions in a routine efficient manner and is not undergoing major change in its functions: for example, the water department in an ordinary city.

The critical systems at any given time are those faced with new demands or new functions because the community is changing. If for example, the water supply runs low, due to drought, population growth, or other circumstances.

Critical Social Systems and some of their Sub-Systems

Educational Systems: Government, private, public school systems, voluntary organisation running system, teachers organisations.

Government Systems: City, district, country level.

Welfare Agency Systems: Welfare Council, Bureau of Public assistance, private charities, settlement houses, youth serving organizations such as YMCA, Scouts, Boys' clubs.

Economic Systems: Banks, departmental stores, industrial corporations, chamber of commerce etc.

Culture Agency Systems: Public Library, Museums, TV and Radio stations, Park districts.

Transportation Systems: Rapid transit, airport, department of streets, expressway systems.

Church Systems: Church federation, Roman catholic, Area or citywide organisations of specific religious denominations.

Civic Organisation Systems: Civil rights organisations, League of women voters, Urban league, Citizens schools organisations.

Supporting Systems: Health maintenance systems, Board of Health, medical societies, hospitals.

Communication: Newspapers, TV and Radio, Telephone systems.

Public Service Systems: Fire, Police, Water Departments, Commission of Human Relations.

Police Organisations

Sociability Systems: Country clubs, "Service" clubs, lodges.

Certain social systems operate effectively when they operate relatively independently. Again the water supply system is an example. It performs a technical and mechanical functions which is clearly defined and it is seldom called upon to cooperate with other systems. On the other hand the educational system is an example of one that must cooperate with other systems, because its functions are complex and similar to the functions of other social systems.

School and Library Systems

The school and the library systems have overlapping functions which are worked out in various ways in different communities.

School and Social Work Agencies

With regard to the different social functions the history of cooperation has been quite different. In western countries many schools provided services to immigrant non-English speaking families (informally done by school principals and teachers working in areas of the city with large immigrant populations. Some schools had "fresh air class rooms" for children with tuberculosis.[7] The attendance of officers in many cases worked with families who needed help. In Chicago some schools began to employ "Visiting teachers" to work with maladjusted children and their families. Many school systems are employing school social workers or visiting teachers, often after a period of cooperation with a social welfare agency which provides and pays the social workers.

In 1960s there was a good deal of experimentation with home school coordinators. There is also some experimentation between public schools and childcare or nursery school agencies to provide pre-school classes for socially disadvantaged children.[8] Gradually, as the schools learn how to make use of social workers and nursery school teachers and if the need for such workers in the schools continues, the schools in the big cities will probably develop social work and nursery school sub-systems of their own.

The Independent School System

The schools should control the administration of all services they perform—even the new and marginal services such as the school lunch programme, recreation services, work experience for job placement of students, transportation. In these an other programmes other social systems have an interest and their personnel may not cooperate if the school system is regarded as unco-operative.

In the present decade there are problems of cooperation in many metropolitan areas between school systems and social welfare agencies, recreation agencies, police and youth-serving agencies and transportation systems.

Frequently the total city government is responsible for social system which might cooperate with a school system. As the city government becomes increasingly responsible for a programme of positive welfare of the city, it comes very close to the activities of the school system.

Co-operative Planning by Social Systems

In a time of social change there is a premium of planning for the future innovation is necessary, and planned innovation gives better results than haphazard innovation.[9] The planning that is needed depends, of course, on the particular social system. With changes in the numbers of people living in the different parts, there is need for planning for new school buildings, churches, libraries, shopping centres etc. with changes in the number of people in various occupations there is need for planning or occupational training programmes and of employment services. At present the need for planning is essential because of two reasons:[10]

1. First, the pace of social change is now so rapid that failure to plan is tantamount to failure of a system to function and,
2. Second, although the vast amount of money is available, are being used in ways that are largely determined at local level. The Central government itself requires a plan

> before releasing money to local Government. This money goes into urban renewal, public housing, education manpower training, highways, health and retirement insurance and cultural activities.

Among private business and private social, cultural and religious systems planning is the accepted procedure.[11] The board of trustees of privately supported colleges assign a planning function to the President of the Institution and often appoints a committee of the board to assist him.

During a period of rapid change it is necessary to have both inter-system and intra-system planning. Inter-system planning involves the school system.

Forms of Inter-System Planning

1. *Employment of Youth*

The economic system no longer employs large number of youths as they reach the school leaving age. At the same time, the secondary schools are not performing efficiently the function of education the kinds of youth who in the past dropped out of schools and went to work. The result is serious youth problem, which is not being handled efficiently.

Recognising the problem, the federal government has supplied money for new kinds of vocational training for youth who are being served by orthodox vocational schools, and has set up major programmes under the job corps and the neighbourhood youth corps. Which social system should receive these funds and take on this new function?

In western countries some school systems are slowly and haltingly developing Urban Youth Programmes to give work experience and to find employment for those youth who are marginal to the labour force and marginal to the school.[12] Some welfare agency systems, such as the YMCA are working at the same task and other youth-serving organizations are setting up work experience and job-finding programmes. Also, some private business firms are accepting government contracts to operate job corps centres to train out of school and unemployed youth. Thus at least three social systems are experimenting with a new function. It is too soon to tell which system can operate best for this purpose, but the channels of inter-systems planning should be kept open during this period of readjustment of function.

Further, after a year or two of work training or work experience the unemployed and marginal youth will be discharged into the labour market at the age of 18 or 19, looking for work. Who will employ them? The state employment office, which are welfare agency systems, have had difficulty placing these youth in the past. Some new way of carrying out the function of providing jobs for youth under it may have to be devised in the current decade. The situation requires inter-system planning between the economic system of employers and employment service, with possibly a government public works agency coming into the picture.

2. *Pre-School Classes*

Another form of inter-system planning is needed in the area of compensatory education for socially disadvantaged children of pre-social age. Cognative development of such children will be marked improved by pre-school education. In Chicago 'Head Start' which began in 1965 are effective. There will be federal and state money to pay for such classes. This new function be taken up by the public school system, by public and private welfare agency systems or by private schools which specialize in this function.

Site Selection and Building Planning

The school system has traditionally planned its own expansion with regard to new sites and buildings. In recent years there has been some inter-system planning between the school system and park systems to bring schools into just position with parks. Now with major programmes of physical urban renewal under way, the city planning agency and the school planning agency have new reasons to cooperate. This is especially important where the goal of urban renewal include the maintenance and stabilization of recially integrated neighbours. The actual location of a new school may be crucial to the stabilisation of an integrated residential area; just as new public and private housing projects will radically affect school attendance patterns. It appears mandatory that school building planning be carried on cooperatively between the school system and the housing system of the community.

Salient Roles in Changing School Systems

The interactions between social systems can be studied in terms of role analysis. The educational system includes among others the following roles:

> Administrator, teacher, Non-professional staff member, Board of Education' members student, parent organization member, civic organization member.

Each of these Roles Represents a Pattern of Behaviour which if a School System is to be successful, is geared smoothly into all the other roles in ways that enable the school to perform its function efficiently and at the same time to provide satisfaction for the people who fill the roles.

The Social Change Occurring: In metropolitan areas are causing many of these roles to undergo rapid redefinition. There are accompanying strains in role performance and in some city school systems accompanying dissatisfactions. The social change which arranged the functions of the school system have also demanded changes in the patterns of behaviour which in an earlier day, where defined as appropriate for the various roles. For example, the teachers role is different if she teaches socially disadvantaged children from what she learned her role should be when she was teaching docile children who were ready learners. Similarly, the principal of an inner-city school has a different role from the one he may have learned earlier as principal of a school in a middle income area. The administrator who has overall charge of a changing system needs a different set of skills and attitudes than the administrator of a stable system in which the school carries out only traditional functions.[13]

At present time is changing in metropolitan areas. There are two roles that are particularly important not only in relation to each other but also in relation to representatives of other social systems: the role of the superintendent and the role of board of education member with regard to other social systems, the role of civic-organization member is a particularly salient one.

The Superintendent Role

Traditionally, the Superintendent's role has consisted mainly of the following behaviours:

1. To discuss matters of policy with the Board of Education generally a member. In most instances, to be careful to yield to the Board in the making of decision, one having

helped to clarify various policy alterntives and their consequences.

2. To select assistant administrators and to divide the work of administration among them.
3. To draw up the annual budget and present it to both the Board and the public.
4. To represent the school system in relation with the public to explain school policies, to hear suggestions and complaints and to persuade the public that the schools are performing their functions well, that the school personnel are working wisely on the problems they are facing.
5. To represent the Board of education in negotiations with teachers and non-professional personnel regarding salaries and working conditions.

In most big cities the role of the Superintendent has three additional major components:

1. To understand the society in which the school operates its social systems and sub-systems and to strive to work out agreement with the other systems on allocations of functions.
2. To plan for the development of the school system, encouraging innovation and evaluation.
3. To analyse the tensions in the community that affect the schools and to work to reduce these tensions by assisting diverse groups to communicate with one another and to achieve a peaceful atmosphere.

The Board Members Role

The Board members role involves the following:

1. To represent the public interest with regard to the school system.
2. To formulate general policy with respect to the curriculum, methods of teaching, organization of the system into sub-districts, placing and building of schools, employment and working conditions of personnel, discipline of students, etc.
3. To conduct independent and continuing scrutiny of the performance of the school system.

4. To determine the financial needs of the school system and to work with appropriate government agencies to secure the needed funds.

The Role of Civic Organisation

Any organization of citizens who have an explicit interest in the school system. Some organisations are city or area wide, some represent a particular segment of the population such as Businessmen or religious leaders or residents of a given local community or neighbourhood. (The present teacher association may be considered a civic organization though its special interests in the schools and its relationship to local schools give its special importance).

The Role of a Member of a Civic Organization Includes the Following Kind of Behaviour[14]

1. To study the school system and attempt to understand its functions and its capabilities.
2. To formulate the educational needs of the particular section of the community which it represents or of the entire community.
3. To communicate with other organizations and attempt to arrive at consensus regarding school policy.
4. To support the Board of Education in its plans for financial support to the schools.

In the period of rapid social change and consequent social conflict, the tendency is for civic organizations to form pressure groups and to promote particular group interests. Thus the year after 1960 have seen the rise of scores of pressure groups in every big city, which express their own needs as they see them.

Role Relations

In the big cities it is inevitable that the role of Superintendent and Board member overlap to some extent. In every city, the Board works out its own arrangement with the Superintendent to provide appropriate separation of duties and maximum accommodation to the particular points of view and particular personalities involved.

The members of the school Board are usually sensitive to the attitudes of the community or certain sections of the community. They are likely to see ways of meeting the desire of the public by adjusting the school programme here and there and by effecting compromises between various pressure groups. They may find themselves dealing with a Superintendent who defines his role in primarily the same terms and who devotes much of the time working with them in adopting policy in the light of total community needs and in promoting good relations with other social systems in the community. On the other hand the Board may find itself at odds with a Superintendent who holds to a more traditional definition of his role; who regards himself as the educational expert; and who concentrates his efforts on problems with in the school system and its sub-systems, rather than upon the relations of the educational system to other social systems of the community.

The pressure groups may separate itself off from the decision-making function, it may assume that a body; such as the board of education, makes the decision and that its own role is to present its case persuasively to that decision-making body, even going to extremes in doing so.

If a city consists of warring factions with respect to school policy and programme, it is unlikely that the Superintendent and the Board of Education can work together in full harmony. The board members will be differentially sensitive to the various pressure groups. The Superintendent may more or less consciously with certain factions in the city.

To illustrate how the roles of school Superintendent, school board member and civic organization member interact the following two hypothetical cases have been constructed—two cities have same problems, same in size, delinquency rates or educational level. In city 'A' the Superintendent has had a wide variety of experience, including class room teaching etc. He spends a great deal of time talking with community leaders and in becoming acquainted with a wide variety of people, encouraging them to tell him freely what they think of the schools. He speaks frequently at public gatherings.

In city 'B' Superintendent also has a vide variety of experience. At one point he announced a plan that would tend to keep experienced teachers. This plan was not discussed with the teachers organisation before it was announced and it met such vociferous opposition from teacher that the Board of Education refused to adopt it. The school system in city 'B' has come to be regarded by representatives of other social systems as cinco-operative. The roles of board members, Superintendent and civic-organization members have become confused in city 'B', the Superintendent has become a controversial figure.

The Indian society is fast changing. Several processes of change are under way to modernize and change the nature and working of our institutions. Educationists and social planners are now thinking seriously to the shape of society and education in the future India. In future India the role of heads, teachers and the School Board will be different. Teachers and administrators should be a radical reformer of the society and education for a creative person and a good co-ordinator of the various systems.

References

1. Persons, Talcott, "The Social System," *Free Press,* 1951, USA.
2. K.C. Panchanadikar and J. Panchanadikar, *Determinants of Indian Social Structure and Social Change in India,* Popular Prakashan, Bombay, 1970.
3. Persons: *Ibid.*
4. Lloyd Allen Cook & Elaive Forsyth Cook, *A Sociological Approach to Education,* 2nd Ed., McGraw Hill Co., New York, 1950.
5. Gore, M.S. & Others, *Papers in the Sociology of Education in India,* NCERT, 1967.
6. Karl Mannhein & Wac Stewart, *An Introduction to the Sociology of Education,* Routeledge & Kegan Paul, London, 1964.
7. Robert J. Stalcup, *Sociology and Education,* Charles E. Merrill Pub. Co., Columbus Ohio, 1968.
8. Charles P. Loomis, *Social Systems: Essay on their Persistence and Changes,* 1960, D. Van Nostrand Co.
9. Bhattacharya—*Society and Education,* Prof. Sriniwas, Calcutta-9, Academic Pub.
10. Brookoner W. B., *A Sociology of Education,* Gott lieb Davia IInd Ed. New York, American Book Co., 1964.
11. Tayler William, *The Sociology of Educational Inequality,* Methuen & Co. Ltd., 1977.
12. Chitnis Suma, *Sociology of Education* (pp. 166-232) in *A Survey of Research in Sociology and Society Anthropology,* Vol. II, Bombay, Popular Prakashan, 1974 (ICSSR).
13. Durkhiem, Emile, *Education and Sociology,* New York, *The Free Press,* 1956.
14. Ottaway, A.K.C., *Education and Society,* Routeledge & Kegan Paul, 1962.

5

Education, Social Stratification and Mobility

Social stratification is a generalized aspect of society and approaches to its study inevitably become a part of larger theoretical constructs. The main approaches to the study of social stratification are the Marxian, Weberian, functional, social-psychological and structuralist.[1] Each of these approaches refer to a specific viewpoint by which structures and processes of social stratification are viewed and patterns of hierarchic social relations are ascertained and valued.

The Indian society may be divided into three main social classes: Upper, middle and lower. The upper class includes very rich businessmen, industrialists, politicians and very highly placed professionals and bureaucrats. They enjoy not only very high economic status and the advantages, but also high social status and political influence. The upper middle class people are usually managers, lawyers, doctors, engineers, professors, highly placed government officers etc. They have lesser socio-economic status than the upper class people, but their style of living approximates to that of the latter.

The middle class people are white-collared workers who have limited resources but high-aspirations to live luxuriously and comfortably like the two classes superior to them. The lower middle class people among whom come school teachers, technicians, clerks and a number of other wage earners doing white-collared and blue-collared jobs, have very tight financial condition but they strive to live, eat, dress and behave like the middle class people.

The lower class people who constitute about 70 per cent of total Indian population are largely made up of agricultural and industrial labourers, low paid employees and daily wage earners, they often suffer from poverty, powerlessness, literacy, disease, hunger, superstition and exploitation of various kinds.

Recent decades have seen the emergence of the new rich upper middle class, among farmers owing large lands and small scale industrialists and traders and that of the new working class, which is generally middle class in industrial and urban areas.

Stratification

On the basis of available data about 80 per cent of our people live in rural areas and 20 per cent in urban areas. Some of the sociological realities of the Indian villages are so distinct that no sensitive social observer of our society can miss them. Even to day our villagers are suffering from poverty, malnutrition, disease, superstitions, traditionalism and caste jealousies, dacoity, thefts agrarian crimes, sex crimes and even murders take place frequently and life is generally insecure and unhappy. Traditional occupations like farming, cattle-farming and cottage industries are still followed, but they are advantageous mostly to those who have large lands or finance such enterprises.

Caste stratification and casteism are very rigidly observed in the villages. The idea of 'Pollution' still debars scheduled castes and many backward classes from going to public wells, temples etc. although winds of social change have been blowing due to the opening of schools, institution of panchayati Raj, influence of electioneering, land-reforms and a number of social legislation measures and the ever-growing rural urban migration. Yet in their actual thinking and behaviour they are still very largely the same sort of dye-hard traditional people as they have been down the centuries'. Due to rising affluence in some sections of rural population, devices like drinking, gambling and litigation and extravagent spending on festivals, rites and modern gadgets have increased all the more.

It is surprising to find that even in villages within a radius of 20 miles of India metropolis, villagers do not have lavatories in their houses as yet, with the result that men, women and children are often seen squatting in nearby fields and along the road side. While many villagers may now boast of their possessions like tractors, radio, television sets, motor cycles, refrigerators and even jeeps and cars, let us not forget that the life of the average villager in India has not improved substantially so far. Despite growing politicization, education of village girls and adults, community development projects etc. sociological studies have revealed that the Indian villages are generally unchanging. The plight of educated youth who have to remain unemployed for many years before they become under-employed, adds to the misery of our villages in which rural industries and modern farming are not properly developed.

The bright side of the Indian urban life shows achievements in terms of higher percentage of literacy, better standard of education, existence of complex institutions, modernising and liberalising values and attitudes of people, greater degree of social interaction in formal groups and associations and sophistication in ways of living and behaviour.

Meaning of Social Stratification

In the words of Young and Mark, "In most societies people classify one another into categories and rank these categories from the higher to lower." The process of defining such category is called 'Social Stratification'.[2] The categories themselves are called strata, popularly they are known as classes.

The rigidity of stratification structure differs in different societies. In some cases it is extremely rigid while in others it is flexible. For example, the caste in Indian society is a very rigid stratification structure. Every member of Hindu society is born into a category known as caste. He can never change his caste. His marriage has to take place with the caste bonds and to a great extent his profession is also decided by his caste affiliation. In many societies the stratification structure is relatively vague and changeable. In such societies the individual's profession or his social status or his marriage partner is not determined on the basis of his birth in a particular category or his belonginging to a particular strata of society. According to Reissman sociologists pose two extreme situations: One in which social positions are ascribed, the other in which social positions are achieved.[3] In the case where social positions are ascribed, rigid divisions are the rule and the separation between strata is unbridgeable. In the case where they are achieved the separation is flexible and social mobility between strata is possible. The class system of America is of the second type while the Indian caste system is of the first type.

Social equality is the basis of social stratification. And all societies, more or less encourage social inequality by stratifying their members. Some sociologists contend that stratification and its resulting inequalities are a necessary, functional requirement of all societies. The society has some highly important functions which are to be performed by its members. It wants that the most capable persons should undertake these functions. It, therefore, distributes these functions among its most talented members. But there are many other functions which are of lower order. Those who perform lower functions; those of labourers or the servants, are placed low in social hierarchy, while those performing the higher functions are placed high in the hierarchy. Thus, the society stratified itself along the lines of its standard of social functions. Which are high and which are low functions are decided by its own evaluative criteria based on value system?

There may be given three types of social characteristics used in stratification systems, considering the fullest spectrum of societies. These are:

1. Such biologically grounded factors as: age, sex, race and kinship;
2. Class characteristics such as occupation, wealth, and power; and
3. any number of idiosyncratic characteristics such as telent and personality.

In any society the stratification may not be based on only any one of these criteria but two or more social characteristics may be mixed together.

Above stratification is described as learning to inequality or as a divisive force in the society. But this is only part of the picture. Stratification also serves as a cohesive social force. If it would have simply remained divisive, all societies were doomed to destruction. Reissman believes that the cohesive element in stratification derives primarily from the social values upon which it depends.[4] The society has certain core-beliefs. The stratification is due to the extension of these core beliefs. Thus, the society's belief system finds an expression in the stratification process.

Since the belief system is an unifying force the society becomes more cohesive through the stratification practised by it.[5] However, there are people in the society who may not subscribe to the divisions in the society. They feel discontent and this discontent can be organized into a force of social change. It may, therefore, be asserted that stratification can mean both divisiveness and cohesion.

Aspects of Stratification

In Indian society stratification may be mentioned along three lines:[6]

1. Stratification on caste basis,
2. Stratification on religion basis, and
3. Stratification on economic class basis.

All the three aspects of stratification are more or less due to ascribed social positions. The religion and caste stratification is purely due to a person being born in a particular religious or caste group. The economic class distinctions are also based on positions at birth. In Indian society the occupations were distributed on caste basis. Even now the scheduled castes by and large take up the same occupations as their forefathers, the Vaish take up business and commerce and the Brahmins the learned professions. Since independence an inter-caste mobility is visible. With the government incentives the members of the lower castes are taking up the vocations of the higher castes. But total impact of such movement is not very high and the societys' occupations are still very much caste-ridden. The lower castes are economically backward and fall in lower class category. Among the occupations of Kshatriya, Vaish and Brahmins there is now more inter-group mobility. These three castes are undertaking various professions and vying with one another in changing their social position. Thus an elite class is being created with the sprinkling of members of all of these three 'Varna' groups. The economic class is thus cutting across the barriers of caste. However, this cutting to a large extent is confined to only three upper castes inspite of all the incentives being given to the lower castes.

Education inters in our country into the picture as stratification and acting more as a divisive force than the cohesive one.[7] In the beginning of the set up of Hindu social structure the stratification might have acted as cohesive force but now such a stratification is leading to various ills in the social order. It is through education that the problem of stratification is now being sought to be solved.

At present Indian society presents a model of closed system in which the range of possible positions, available to an individual are fixed by a set of status transmission and marriage rules. In such a system the individual's position is determined by the position of his family. Individual himself has only limited opportunity to either rise or fall in the hierarchy. This model has to be changed through education into a model of the 'open-system' in which the only restriction upon movement in and out of positions are determined by the abilities of the individual himself. But for achieving this model, equality of educational opportunities must be provided. In Indian situation this is happening in the form of public schools. The intellectual elite which has gained higher positions during the British regime wishes to transfer their statuses and positions to their children by providing them education in public schools where predominantly an education in English patterns through English medium is given.[8] The sons of ordinary citizens fail to send their children to these schools which are very expensive and thus are deprived of quality education through English medium. Still the official language of the land is English and it is also the language of big business. Thus a typical situation exists in the Indian society. On the one hand, efforts are being made to cut barriers of stratification along the caste lines, on the other, more stratification on class lines is being inculcated through a class conscious educational system.

Social Mobility

When a person serving at a lower job moves to a job which provides him higher position and status he has altered his position in the class structure. According to Young and Mark: 'Social Mobility' means movement within the social structure.[9] When a person achieves a different type of education from that of his parents or moves into a different occupational status or adopts a different style of life he may be considered to be socially mobile. According to Sorokin Social Mobility deals with a change in social position of persons and groups in social change.[10]

Social Mobility may be of two types:

1. Vertical, and 2. Horizontal.

An alteration in status upwards or downwards is considered as indicative of Vertical Mobility. Horizontal mobility is a movement from one status to another when there is no difference between the ranks of the two statuses,[11] for example a person who is a farm labourer when becomes an industrial labourer has only moved horizontally. A son of a sweeper when goes to the school, graduates and gets a high government job, has moved upward in status. This movement is vertical because this mobility is from the status position into which he was born.

Factors Affecting Social Mobility

The following factors influence social Mobility:

1. *Education:* Those persons who receive more and more education achieve higher social status. This gives an impetus to the growth of social mobility in a formal and natural way.
2. *Aspirational Level:* The more ambitious the people in a society the more social mobility grows.
3. *Opportunity Structure:* Opportunity received by a person powerfully influences the process of social mobility. Through education and progressive democratic ideas in India now caste rigidity is loosing and the path of social mobility is getting free of the stronghold of caste system.
4. *Demographic Structure:* Birth rate and migration of village folk towns and cities are closely connected to social mobility. When people migrate to places of greater density of population than their higher status gladly accept even menial jobs and thus local population rises to higher status. After independence revolutionary progress has occurred in India in the field of industry as well as agriculture. More and more people are migrating to cities and industrial centres from villages to take jobs in factories and mills. This has greatly promoted social mobility.
5. *Economic Success:* Each individual irrespective to his group strives more and more to earn more and more money in order to achieve higher status and social prestige. Their economic success influence their social mobility from one group to another group.
6. *Occupational Improvement:* Some occupations are associated with great social status and prestige in comparison with

others. In our country occupational improvement is increasing day-by-day and, therefore, the social mobility is also going up.

Education and Social Mobility

Education abolishes social rigidity, removes discrimination based on birth and destroys rigid stratification. It also strives to achieve higher ideals, obtains higher positions of prestige, formation of good habits and inculcation of permanent values.[12] Education is also helping to develop ability and capacity in the individual to gain higher statuses, prestige and promotes effective social mobility. Promotion and higher position provides a teacher higher mobility. More education provides students higher social status.

Education is capable to promote the growth and remove the backwardness of a country. It can contribute to the social awakening among people.

Education creates a divide between the educated and the uneducated people. This divide makes a society unequal. The educated become a class by itself as they have an access to white-coller jobs and channels of upward social mobility. Educated middle class consists of upper and middle caste, clusters and the form of managers, teachers, doctors, engineers, clerks, administrators etc. According to Krishna Kumar, "education reproduces elites by circumventing the opportunities to education and subsequently to the positions of high status and power."[13]

In some countries, where more useful and productive work in the education, the more is social mobility because only capable children will go up whereas the incapable and mentally retarded will go down. Education will achieve both these processes and attain a balance between the two kinds of mobility—upward and downward. The belief that upward mobility in both possible and desirable is called the 'Mobility ethic'. This ethic is very clearly visible in the advanced countries, while it is almost absent in the backward countries.

In India the religious tradition, the faith in easy going life and shunning of material gains have resulted in much of stiffing of a desire for vertical mobility. Contentment with scarcity has been a norm here and therefore, the society as a whole has suffered. Education can help in altering this situation. It may bring changes in the norms and value-patterns. It can create a climate for hard work. But the opportunities for education to the lower classes in

India are very limited particularly in rural areas. The prevalent value-system governs their aspirations and actions. On the basis of different researches, the low classes do not aspire for higher education due to the realisation of the existing situation or due to some impact on their personality patterns of the prevailing value structure. Therefore, it is an urgent need that educational facilities must be extended for lower class and other backward sections of the society.

Through education there should provision to prepare all the individuals for vocations and create a confidence in earning one's own living. The more stress should lay on women's education. It is in the interest of the society to provide the maximum educational opportunities and in return make use of the best talent available in the service of the society by giving them due reward.

References

1. Sharma, K.L., *Social Stratification in India: Issue and Themes*, Sage Publication, New Delhi, 1997.
2. Kimball, Young and Raymond W. Mark, *Sociology and Social Life*, American Book Co., New York, 1962, p. 168.
3. Leonard Reissman, *Social Stratifications in Sociology* edited by Nail J. Smelser, John Wiley, New York, 1967, pp. 208-10.
4. Sorokin, P.A., "Social and Cultural Mobility", *The Free Press*, Illinois, 1927, p. 3.
5. Gore, M.S. and Desai, I.P. (ed.), *Papers in Sociology of Education India*, NCERT, 1971.
6. Mathur, S.S., *A Sociological Approach to Indian Education*, Vinod Pustak Mandir, Agra, 1971.
7. Dube, S.M., *Social Mobility among the Professions: Study of Professions in a Traditional Indian City (Gorakhpur, U.P.)*, Popular Prakashan, Bombay, 1975, pp. 76-77.
8. Dube: *Ibid.*
9. Herbert H. Hyman; "The Value Systems of Different Classes: A Social Psychological Contribution to the Analysis of Stratification", in Reinhard Bendix and Seymor M. Lipset, eds; "Class Status and Power"; The Free Press, New York, 1951.
10. Sorokin: *Ibid.*
11. Richard M. Stephenson, *Mobility Orientation and Stratification: A Study of One Thousand Ninth Graders*, unpublished doctoral dissertation, Columbia University, New York.
12. Bernard, Barber, *Social Stratification*, Harcourt Brace & Co., New York, 1957.
13. Pandey, Prem Narain, *Education and Social Mobility*, Daya Publishing House, Delhi, 1988.

6

Education and Social Change

The rapid development of science and technology have inevitably created a superculture and this in turn has created a tragic situation for the developing and the under-developed countries. These under-developed countries try to adopt the models of economic, social, political, cultural and educational developments from the highly developed countries which have started taking a leap forward into the atomic and electronic age and thus the gap between the under-developed and the highly developed has become wider instead of getting narrow. It is quite significant to note that the efforts made by the under-developed countries appear hesitant and inconsistent.[1] However, these countries should concentrate all their developmental efforts towards the fulfilment of the two main objectives—renationalisation and modernisation—through an effective process of national reconstruction of their ideologies, cultures, administration, economic, social and educational structures. In the accomplishment of this task the international cooperation has become obligatory practically in every field of national development as it is not possible for any country developed or under-developed to solve its problems and workout their salvation atonce and unaided. Re-nationalisation implies an attachment or return to certain traditional elements of the national character which are essential for the preservation of the national identity, while the process of modernisation implies the adoption of some progressive and innovatory changes in the traditional way of life. This causes situation of internal contradition and the resulting failure on the part of the under-developed countries in pursuing their developmental programmes. Whatever is traditional has been discarded and whatever is going to replace it has not so far been fully created, accepted and assimilated.

Another significant feature of the change is that the third world countries, when they emerged from the colonial domination, started their whole-hearted endeavours in fighting against ignorance which they viewed as an essential condition for the preservation of freedom and the national development. But their increasing investment in education exceeded the limits of their financial resources and the production of the educated and trained persons increased more than their economic structures could absorb them and this has caused a problem of unemployment. On the other hand there are some progressive countries which are increasingly adopting more innovations, practices and are ceaselessly improving their institutions and structures. Yet, these affluent nations cannot afford to neglect the ignorant, the hungry and the destitute as in the rapidly changing modern world it is becoming highly desirable to end all types of disparities and inequalities—social, political, economic and civil etc. and to provide a minimum level of standard of living to all people irrespective of their race, creed, nationality, religion and birth.

The industrial scientific and technological revolutions, has placed all our life-problems and way of living in a quite new perspective, giving us entirely new ways of thinking and acting on the universal basis irrespective of the nature of country—developed or developing. The mass communication media has provided the political, economical and educational authorities with an extra-ordinary instrument for conditioning the individual and the society.

The technological era brought new hopes and bright prospects for the future prosperity and happiness of human life but at the same time it also entails some of the dangers such as over population, exhaustion of power and food resources, pollution of water and air, the invention of intelligence-destroying chemicals and the nuclear weapons, capable of destroying the whole human race.

Due to above developments there are some social changes going on all over the world. These changes affect the whole personality and life style of the persons.

What is 'Social Change'?

Social change is the variation and modification in any aspect of social process, pattern of form. Kingslay Davis defines it as "only such alterations as occur in social organisation, i.e. in the structure and functions of society,"[2] Johnson[3] covers five kinds of changes under social change:

1. Change in social values,
2. Institutional change,
3. Change in distribution of possessions and rewards,
4. Change in personnel, and
5. Change in abilities or attitudes of personnel.

According to Moris Ginsberg; Social Change implies a change in social structure, e.g., the size of society, the composition or balance of its parts or the type of its organisations. Examples of such changes are the contraction in the size of family or a domestic unit which occurred in many societies.[4] In the words of Kuppuswamy, "When we speak of social change we simply assert that there is some change in social behaviour and in the social structure."[5]

In each and every sort of variation, modification or change in an individuals behaviour in society cannot be called social change. In order to qualify to be called social change a variation or change fairly lasting or significant, it should also set a trend and revealed in the social relations, behaviour, values or actions of a good number of people in the society. Social changes affects a wide range of individual experience and functional aspects of society.

Meaning of Planned Change

According to Wills H. Griffin and Udai Pareek; "planned change is the organised effort of the leadership of a country to bring about improvement in one or more aspects of their society. It involves the careful management of resources and effort to bring about change of a particular nature, moving in a particular direction."[6] Planned change includes thoughtful consideration of the steps required to bring about the desired improvements, the techniques and methods to be used to accomplish each step and the decisions to be made to provide the needed resources and to channel effort in support of the required steps.[7] For successful planned change the planners and leaders of change must have a clear idea about the improvement and changes. The best example of planned change in our country is formulation and implementation of the Five Year Plans. Because these plans deal with agricultural productivity, industrial growth, hydro-electric power projects, population control, international trade, handicrafts, small-industry development, village and community development, local government, health, expansion of education and many other areas of Indian life.

Indian development schemes and programmes represent planned attempts to bring about change in a particular direction and a large number of projects sponsored by Central and state agencies for the improvement of education are a part of the overall effort to bring about planned growth.

Process of Change

The term "process of change" suggests an orderly, organised step-wise series of actions, will result in achieving desired process of development. The process of change is gradual, piecemeal, and incidental. It may be slow, slower in some societies than others, but it is continuous and contiguous. Each change grows out of the situation before it, and it contributes to changes that follow. If the process of change is neither easy to understnad nor to guide.

If the process of change is clearly definable and predictable, then the task of the planners and leaders of change would be easy one. To an increasing degree of the planners and administrators of development projects and scholars of change process are working together, exchange of experience among developmental workers in various areas such as community development and education, certainly educational workers can profit from the experience of other workers from whom they have been relatively isolated during the early period of Indian development.

Patterns of Social Change

Social change have some significant features. They may be planned changes or unplanned changes. They may be caused by internal factors or by external factors. According to MacIver and Page there may be three patterns of social change:[8]

1. *Cumulative Change:* The later developments are based upon the earlier developments, therefore, it can be pictured as a curve which is going upwards.

2. *Change in one Direction Followed by the Reverse Direction:* In some aspects there is a change in the upward direction but afterwards there is a reversal of direction. For example international trade may advance and then fall off.

3. *Wave-like Change:* It is like the second patterns, but there is no continuous increase even for some time. It is more like a wave with its alternating ups and downs. Fashions in society often follow the pattern.

The course of change may be gradual or rapid, peaceful or violent, continuous or spasmodic, orderly or erratic. The magnitude of change may be small or large. Social changes are usually complex. It is difficult to predict which direction or directions a certain change will take and what sort of changes it will lead to. Social change is a universal phenomenon, it occurs in all societies.

Factors Responsible for Social Changes

Social changes are caused by several factors. Physical factors or factors related to nature like earth-quakes, volcanoes, floods and fire may render people homeless and rescind, turning them into refugees, forced to change their whole style of living by migrating to other places.[9]

1. *Demographic factors:* Like imbalance caused by change in ratio of males and females in a given population can lead to social changes, for example large numbers of young male soldiers died in Europe during World War II. The number of girls and women increased over the existing number of males and this lead to moral deterioration and sexual permissiveness throughout the Europe.

2. *Political Factors:* Like World War II, rule of Nizé dictator, Hitler in Germany, Bangladesh crisis and partition of India in 1947 have brought about several social changes in the respective societies.

3. *Economic Factors:* Like poverty, inflation, the Green Revolution and large amount of money remitted to their families by Indians serving abroad certainly bring about a lot of social change in their behaviour, relations, spending patterns, institutions and outlook of the world.

4. *Industrial Factors:* Like establishment of industrial townships, urbanisation and trade unionism are responsible for several kinds of social changes the lives of the people concerned.

5. *Scientific Technological Inventions and Discoveries:* They have caused several far-reaching social changes in the lives of people in developing as well as developed countries. Radio, television, refrigerator, car, aeroplanes, new household gadgets etc. have completely changed our style of living. Modes of thinking and social relations and even morals.

6. *Social and Cultural Factors:* Like fashions, women's liberation movement, renaissance or reformist movements and Satyagraha, definitely cause a lot of social change in diverse directions.

Relationship Between Education and Social Change

Education in our society increasingly concerned with the indigenous regional differences with urban and rural variety and with the rapidly developing multi-racial and multi-cultural elements. There is also the additional problem of fragmented and fragmentary sub-cultures, which arise suddenly and almost as suddenly die, change or become transformed or subsumed in the main cultural stem.[10] Change of any sort is very painful to many people who have established their own norms, standards and concepts of stability. The relationship between education and social change may be of three types.

1. Education as a Condition for Social Change

The first form of relationship emphasises that without the basis, foundation or ground of education, no desired social structure or place of social change can be erected. There must be education as a basic condition and only that can any real social change or modernisation be possible. If properly educated and well trained workers are not available to handle that sort of modern machinery, it is bound to cause several grave losses and dangers.[11] One can witness such examples in the factories and mills in India where illiterate, semi-literate and ill-trained workers are meeting numerous failures in increasing the quality and quantity of the goods produced by them and thereby, bringing about no real social change, modernisation, progress or improvement in the existing situation.

Similarly, Sharda Marriage Act and other reform programmes are more or less at a superficial level due to lack of education.

Our Constitution-makers had rightly realised the importance of education and therefore, they had emphatically laid down in the constitution that the state shall be obliged to provide free and compulsory education up to elementary level to all its citizens within a few years of the implementation of the Constitution.

2. *Education As An Instrument of Social Change*

A society wishing to change itself has to employ a number of instruments, institutions, agents or agencies to achieve its desired goals. Among such means, education is perhaps the most important. It will provide necessary training in skills and occupations and produce the needed competent personnel for manning the different specialised jobs in modern industrial, business, educational, research establishment and secondary associations. It is also expected to change the values and attitudes of people and to create in them an urge and the necessary motivation to achieve social class ascendency, social mobility and their Sanskritization.

It is now widely held that modern education can mould people into enlightened, empathetic, risk-taking, thick skinned, industrious and mobile personalities. That education will be of an immense help in bringing about democratisation, secularism, national integration as well as economic prosperity and proper political socialisation in the given country. It is generally believed by the people that axe of education can cut down the thick roots of traditions, superstitions, ignorance, backwardness, parochialism etc.

Education is one of the most important tools of drastic change like social revolution. Effectiveness of this tool is to depend on the following things:

1. The purpose of education must be clearly defined.
2. Education must emphasize social reform.
3. Teachers who are going to be the active agents for bringing about the change are properly enlightened and trained.
4. The teachers' have themselves to become mobile personalities with high degree of empathy, achievement, motivation, social sensitivity, risk taking capability and similar other attributes of a modern man.

3. *Education as the Effect of Social Change*

When certain major social changes set in a society, one of their effects or consequences generally is that people become conscious of the importance of getting education of receiving higher academic and professional training of changing their values, attitudes and behaviour by critically assessing their modes of socialisation and then modifying them suitably and doing things like that. If we recall the development of urbanisation and industrial townships in India during this century we can easily present several evidences to show that they have greatly stimulated the enrolment of students, both boys and girls in primary and secondary schools, colleges, professional and vocational institutions in the villages and towns situated on the fringes of these new cities and industrial townships. An era of democratic decentralisation in rural India commencing since 1959 has greatly stimulated education in all sections of the people at least in terms of quantity, not in quality.

The Agent of Change in Education

Every culture has had saints, revolutionaries and public men of vision who worked for reform and advancement in their society. India has a rich tradition of agents of change of all shades and kinds. Some saints have been soft-spoken, e.g. Tukaram in Maharashtra, Tyagaraja in Tamilnadu and Bharati in Karnatak, but persuasive agents who commanded considerable influence among their people. On the other hand persons such as Kabir have been more outspoken, scathingly criticising the prevalent order of authority, mocking common practices and yet being listened to and making an impact. One could also mention many teachers from several periods of Indian history, who have worked effectively for change. We can take the example of Mahatma Gandhi, Vinobha Bhave and other personalities.

To perform some important tasks successfully, for example helping communities and groups to planout development or reform objectives to focus on problem situations to seek possible solutions, to arrange for assistance, to plan action intended to improve situations, to overcome the difficulties in the way of productive action and to evaluate the results of planned effort, the agent of change requires certain personal qualities, certain knowledge, understanding and certain skills. He needs to have an understanding of human dynamics of evolutionary development and a philosophically sound concept of his job in working with them. Most of all, he must understand that his responsibility is to help others learn to help themselves.

There are few agents of change in Indian education, in the

pure sense. Few positions have been established for this purpose and few persons in other kind of positions find themselves able to perform the change entry role. The coordinators of extension centres, the staff of the State Institute of Education and the staff of certain other state and central government agencies may be viewed as change agents. The University or higher education institute professor who is invited to work with a particular school improvement project, may behave as an agent of change while he is serving as a resource person or consultant.

The main goal of change agent is to bring about change in his clients, individually and organisationally. His interest should be in primary and in particular programmes, projects, schemes or changes in the school system should be secondary. He may promote worthwhile innovations for their own sake, but his focus should be on using them to develop in the client system certain characteristics that will enable it to become innovating in its own right, with a minimum of outside prompting and assistance. A person who is changeprone is inquisitive, anxious to improve, experimental in outlook, positively critical of himself, cooperative with others in discussing problems and professionally alert. The change agent needed sensitive abilities such as ability to take criticism, to admit error, to be self critical, to suspend judgement, to ask for assistance, to take initiative, to make choices between alternatives, to contribute to group morale, to make and carryout decision and to work harmoniously with difficult individuals. The agent of change should accept responsibility for helping to develop both the general skills needed and the specific technical skills and abilities related to particular innovations. The change agent should let the client system independent on him. They must develop a sense of independence and ability to "Stand on their own feet." This is more important in carrying on the continuing process of change and innovation than in carrying out routine duties. The agent must work in such a way that he provides the minimum rewards to assure successful experimentation.

To achieve his goals the agent of change perform certain functions. The agent of change in education should be a generalist in education, not attempting to provide answers on all problems but having a broad interest in and understanding of educational programmes, their purposes and operations. In addition, he should be a specialist in one or more areas. He should play, has to do with promoting and initiating school improvement programmes.

The agent should provide community experiences for his students which requires the cooperation of government and private agencies in the community. He rewarded persons who did outstanding work but tried never to punish or criticise publicity any of the less active personnel: The change agent should himself exemplify willingness to change and grow through experience. He should be change-prone and innovative in his own work.[12]

We have briefly discussed the rapid development, their feature, meaning of social change, patterns of social change, factors responsible and relationship between education and social change. All aspects are very important. If the progress of the Indian nation has continued to remain arrested in the whirlpool of traditional discriminations, parochialism, poverty, unemployment, youth unrest, political immaturity, aversion to change and dysfunctions like these fifty years of education planning at a grand level, it is high time when all those concerned with the survival and progress of the largest democracy of the world, must seriously consider how education in India can be remodelled, reformed and revitalised and how our strategies of using this potential tool should change, so that the message of social change may not only be conveyed but become a practical reality in all spheres of life.

References

1. UNESCO, *Learning To Be*, Sterling Publishers, New Delhi, 1973, p. 40.
2. Davis Kingslay, *Social Process and Change*, New York.
3. Johnson, Ray Earl, *Confronting Organisational Change*, Association Press, New York, 1963.
4. Ginsberg, Moris, *Social Change*, British Journal of Sociology.
5. B. Kuppuswamy, *Social Change in India*, Vikas Publishers, New Delhi, 1972, p. 9.
6. Griffin H. Willis and Pareek Udai, *The Process of Planned Change in Education*, Somaiya Publishers, Bombay, 1970.
7. Gore, M.S., Desai, I.P., *Papers in the Sociology of Education in India*, NCERT, New Delhi, 1967.
8. Maclver and Page, *Sociology*, p. 29.
9. Ruhela (Ed.), *Social Determinants of Educability in India*, Papers in the Sociological Context of Indian Education, Jain Brothers, New Delhi, 1969.
10. Shah, B.V., *Gujarat Students and Social Change*, M.S. University, Baroda, 1965.
11. Srinivas, M.N., *Education and Social Change*, T.A., Mathias (ed.) Jusuit Education Association, Delhi, 1968.
12. Cormack, Margaret, *She Who Rides Peacock: Indian Students and Social Change*, Asia Publishing House, Bombay, 1961.

7

Education and the Goal of Secularism

The term 'secular' means 'non-spiritual', having no concern with religious or spiritual matters, anything which is opposed to, or not connected with religious or ecclesiastical things, temporal as well as opposed to spiritual or ecclesiastical. According to Eric S. Walter secularism is an ideology which provides a theory of life and English dictionary secularity denotes the absence of connection with religion, secular literature means literature that is not concerned with or devoted to the service of religion.[1]

Likewise secular education means a curriculum where religious education is excluded and a secularist attitude is one which progressively tends to isolate religion from the stood terms, secularism signifies the separation of the state and the church. Smith well defines it thus, "The secular state is a state which guarantees individual a corporate freedom of religion, is not constitutionally connected to a particular religion."[2] The word "secularism" was first used in the nineteenth century by George Jacob Holydake. He derived it from the Latin word 'seculum' meaning 'this present age' and used it in the context of social and ethical values or system. Thus secularism came to be known as a social and ethical system based on the following principles evolved by Holydake:

1. Principle of primary emphasis on the material and cultural improvement of human beings.

2. Principle of respect for search for all truth, whatever be its source, which can be tested in experience leading to human betterment.
3. Principle of concern for this age or world and its improvement.
4. Principle of an independent rational morality, which does not base itself on faith in divine commandment.

Indian conception of secularism requires that there shall be no state religion and the state shall treat all religion equally. In the words of Mahatma Gandhi, "we believe in Sarva-Dharma-Samantava having equal regard for all faiths and creeds."

Indian Constitution and Secularism

The idea of secularism is boldly traceable in the basic frame work of the Constitution having in its first indication in the preamble and its elaborate manifestation in various fundamental rights relating to equality, freedom, religion, education and culture. The ideal of secularism, as embodied in the Constitution, is based on the principle to which the Congress party under Mahatma Gandhi remained so irrevocably wedded. A leading member Ananthasayaanam Ayyangar stated in the Constituent Assembly on December 7, 1948 "we are pledged to make the state a secular one. I do not by the word secular mean that we do not believe in any religion, and that we have nothing to do with it in our day-to-day life. It only means that the state or the Government cannot aid one religion or give preference to one religion as against another."[3] The secular character of our Constitution is traceable in these important directions.

The preamble declares India a secular state and speaks of the liberty to all citizens in religion to various important matters that includes faith, belief and worship.

> ***Art. 15(1) and** (2)* says that the state shall not discriminate against any citizen on various grounds in which, religion, race and caste have their conspicuous place. It is, further provided that on several grounds (including those of religion, race and caste) no citizen can be subjected to any liability or disability with regard to access to shops, public restaurants, hotels and places of public entertainment and the use of wells, tanks, bathing ghats, roads and places of public resort wholly or partly maintained by the state.

Art. 16 (1) and (2) says that no citizen on several grounds like those of religion, race or caste, among others, shall be intelligible for, or discriminated against, in matters of public employment, nor shall he be denied admission into any educational institution wholly or partly maintained by the state.

Art. 17 says that untouchability is abolished and its practice in any form is forbidden, the enforcement of any arising out of untouchability shall be offence punishable under the law.

Art. 25 (1) says that all persons are equally entitled to freedom of conscience and have right to profess, practise or propagate any religion.

Art. 26 provides that every religious denomination or any section thereof shall have the right to establish and maintain institutions for religious and charitable purposes, to manage its own affairs in matters of religion, to own and acquire movable and immovable property, and to administer such property in accordance with law.

Art. 27 says that no person shall be compelled to pay any taxes the proceeds of which are specifically appropriated in payment of expenses for the promotion or maintenance of any particular religious denomination.

Art. 28 provides that no religious instruction shall be provided compulsorily in any educational institution wholly or partly maintained by the state.

Art. 29 and 30 provide that state shall not impose upon it any culture other than community's own culture[4] and every community shall have the right to establish and administer educational institution of its choice and the state shall not, in granting aid to educational institutions discriminate against such an educational institution maintained by a majority community on the ground that it is under the management of a religious community.

All these provisions of the Constitution boldly declare that India is a secular state. As Basu says "The sum total of the above provision makes our state more secular than even the United States of America."

In 42nd Amendment Act, 1976 the preamble was amended and two new words were added to the first section of it, which reads thus—

"We, the people of India, having solemnly resolved to constitute India into a sovereign socialist, secular and democratic Republic and to secure to all its citizens."[5]

By enshrining it in the preamble we have merely inscribed into our fundamental law and accepted fact, secularism in our country does not mean anti-ecclesiasticism. It only signifies what the Congress president D. K. Barooah in his inaugural address delivered at the convention on Constitutional Amendments in New Delhi on October 16, 1976 said that "we have respect for all religions and equal respect for all. Respect for religion does not depend on the number of the people that follow the religion. All religion in this country, however, shall their strength may be, have the same status and same prestige and same support from the state."[6] On the same occasion, then Union Law Minister H.R. Gokhale defined this concept as: "There will be freedom, liberty of faith and worship whatever religion you belong to, is all what you mean by secularism."[7] All that does mean is that the state will not have anything to do as a state with any religion excepting to treat every religion equally, but the state will not have any foundation of religion.

Hunter Commission 1882

Hunter Commission recommended encouragement to indigenous schools and declared "All indigenous schools whether high or low, should be recognised and encouraged if they serve any purpose of secular education whatsoever."[8]

This shows that even before independence secularism was in the mind of some Indians.

Education Commission (1964-66)

Education Commission (1964-66) with regard to education on social, moral and spiritual value Art. 8.95 said that a sense of purpose should inspire all school activities and must be reflected in the life, tone and atmosphere of the school, the school assembly, the curricular and co-curricular activities, the celebration of religious festivals of all religions.

Art. 8.9: In this article Education Commission gives the relation between the moral values and religion. There must be correlation between the moral values sought to be inculcated and the teachings of great religions, stories drawn from the great religions and discuss the moral values and problems in life. All religions stress certain fundamental qualities of character such as honesty and truthfulness consideration for others, reverence for old age, kindness to animals and compassion for the needy and the suffering. In the literature of every religion the story or parable figures prominently as a means of impressing an ethical values on the followers. The narration of such stories by the teachers at the right moment in the programme of moral education would be more effective particularly in the lower classes.

Art. 8.98: Some of the great religious and spiritual leaders may be included in the study of social studies or literature but it is essential that all important religions are represented properly in the programme. Similarly the celebration of the festivals of different religions will afford opportunities for narration of incidents from the life history of leaders of these religions.

National Policy on Education 1986

Art. 8.5 of NPE 1986 sub-headed by value education says that in our culturally plural society, education should foster universal and eternal values, oriented, towards the unity and integration of our people.[9]

Such value education should help eliminate obscurantism, religious fanaticism, violence, superstition and fatalism.

Review of National Policy on Education 1990

Report of the committee for review of National Policy on Education 1990, entitled "Towards an enlightened and humane society" also says that education is a multi-dimensional process, while developing the individual, there must also be a stress on education contributing to assist the students towards attaining national goals and purposes.[10] There is a widespread feeling among a cross-section of the people in India today that all is not well with our body politic and that education must contribute actively and positively to find a part of the solution, currently national unity and secularism, scientific temper and humane and caring society and among the pressing national goals. The report of the National Commission on Teachers (1983-85)[11] mentions the following four national goals—

— A united secular India

— A modern nation
— A productive people
— A humane and caring society

Having emphasised on the common school system the report says that the implication of having the common school system has been stated by the policy to be gaining of access to education of a comparable quality by all students irrespective of caste, creed location or sex.

Thus all the above mentioned commissions and policies put much stress on secularism in education. Nevertheless none of these have said that the students should not be taught religion. All have very clearly said that school children must be taught the religious values through the religious stories and great spiritual leaders. But the sad thing is that in most of the schools in India even the moral values are not taught to the students. The great spiritual leaders are taught in social science but only with the point of view of their examination and therefore the spiritual values of those leaders are often unknown to pupils. Thus secularism remains in theory.

Need of Secular-Based Education

A country like India needs secular-based education because of many reasons:

1. Development of Moral Outlook

Secular based foundation for development of character and moral development. It inculcates in students humanity, truthfulness, tolerance, honesty, courtesy, sympathy, spirit of service and sacrifice which form a noble character of man and develops his personality. Hence secular-based education is essential for developing moral character of students.

2. Development of Wider Attitude

Secular based education is required to make a man dynamic and enlightened, to develop in him a wider attitude towards life and to take interest in social service by sacrificing his selfish motive. It can make him courageous enough to face the problems of life boldly and solve them to the best of his efforts and intelligence.

3. Development of Democratic Qualities

This education is very much needed as it helps man in developing democratic qualities like liberty, equality, fraternity and cooperative living. True secularism stresses the dignity of the individual and the sacredness of human personality. Secular education helps to establish and incorporate democratic process. If true secularism is taught then every person will be treated as an end and every as means only.

4. Development of Futuralistic Outlook

It fosters the growth of science, art, philosophy and even religion. A pluralistic outlook is the very essence of democracy and fortunately in India, the secular approach to life has engendered it.

5. Cultural Development

It preserves and reinforces culture. Both secularism and culture go hand in hand and influence each other. Secularism is a dynamic aspect of culture and it must have place in the curriculum.

6. Development of Specific Spirit

The scientific spirit releases the individual from strong bonds of blind faith. The scientific spirit implies a spirit of free enquiry, a spirit of looking at things, objectively and rationally freedom from an obsession with the past and a more humble attitude towards our own history and achievements. Secular based education promotes such scientific values as rationality, objectivity and open mindedness apart from humanistic values like tolerance and compassion.

7. Balance Between Spiritual and Material

Secular based education glorifies material needs and promotes reverence for earthly life, without rejecting spiritual values. Secularism is based on certain fundamental human values, and looks upon science not merely as a means of material progress but a quest for truth and a search for harmony with nature.

8. Basis of Humanitarianism

Secular based education is the basis of humanitarianism. It stands for peace, goodwill and understanding. It helps in fostering the brotherhood of man and the unity of the world. It is felt that the absence of secular education has caused exploitation, and corruption, disaster, selfishness, aggression and hatred in the world. There is a chaos and disorder. Betterment of the world depends upon secular based education. It will raise man to a high level. It will encourage the policy of live and let live and provides the basis of true humanitarianism. It will help in replacing hatred in love, selfishness in self-sacrifice and violence in non-violence, secular based education will cause happiness, order and contentment in the world by cultivating faith in truth, beauty and goodness.

The adoption of the policy of secularism raises some vital issues of education, such as—

1. How education might promote secularism and develop secular attitudes?
2. To take note of the psychological and social factors that work against secularism in education.
3. What is the place of religion in education in a state committed to secularism?
4. Can morals and values be taught without reference to real religion? If yes? How?

People differ in their opinion on all these points. In the past religion and education were very closely linked in most countries, religious institutions undertook the task of education. The situation became very different when the responsibility of education shifted from religious institutions to the state. In 1939 the England Consultative Commission on secondary education said— "There is a wide and genuine recognition of the value and importance of religious institution and no boy or girl can be counted as properly educated unless he or she has been made aware of the existence of a religious interpretation of life."[12]

As substantial number of people favourably disposed towards religion, nevertheless believe that any religious teaching in schools is inappropriate and that it should be left to the family and religious institution, schools, instead of teaching religion might safely teach about religion, about the major religions of the society and about religion as a social force.

Instead of value based on the religion they could teach the values of democratic way of life, values derived from social ideologies could be taught to serve the purpose. There are some secularists who see no place for any religion in the school. They would seem to be in agreement with those who firmly believe in man's capacity to solve his own problems and evolve his own value system without the help of religion.

History and experience gave evidence that for the individual religion could be a great source of moral and spiritual strength and for the society a strong social force. Therefore, the University Education Commission (1948-49) and Sri Prakas Committee on Religious and Moral Instruction in 1959[13] were set up to look into the provisions of religious and moral instruction in schools:

1. Instruction based on all important religions was to be given, important principles of all religions should be taught.
2. Teachers themselves should set examples of good moral conduct.
3. A suitable climate should be created in schools through prayers, meditation, reading from religious text etc.
4. Religious tolerance must be taught.

The Kothari Commission also stressed the need for the inculcation of right values in students at all stages and to introduce education in moral, social and spiritual values. The Commission emphasised that teaching of moral, social, spiritual values do not go against the spirit of secularism. Therefore, secularism is not irreligious or anti-religious policy. It gives everyone the full freedom of religious faith and worship and is anxious to promote not only religious tolerance but also an active reverence for all religions.

Educational Efforts for Promotion of Secularism

Our educational system today promotes secular attitudes and values through its broad-based aims, curricula, enlightened teachers and appropriate activities, all emphasising open-mindedness, progressivism, rationality, freedom from bigotry and superstition, and equal respect for all religions.

1. Educational Aim

Our educational aims and objectives are secular. They seek to develop our nation as a rational, democratic, progressive and modern welfare state. The philosophy of humanism guides our educational objectives. The well-being of all the citizens of the country is the goal towards which all our educational energies are directed.

2. *Organisation of Educational Institutions*

The organisation of most of our educational institutions is based on secular principles. In all government institutions and government aided institutions, it is necessary to observe secular, democratic, rational criteria in appointments, promotions, admissions and all such matters.

3. *Educational Curricula*

Our educational curricula at all levels lays special emphasis on the promotion of secular values. Lessons in text-books are free from religious bigotry and prejudices while the good ideas and values emphasised in different religions are presented in appropriate forms. All co-curricular activities aim at promoting harmony culture in the students. It is not permitted in the course of any instructional or co-curricular activity to condemn or unduly praise any one particular religious or cultural system or institution. It is the usual practice in all schools, colleges and Universities to celebrate fairs, festivals, birth anniversaries etc. relating to different religions. Equal importance is given to different faith while imparting moral education.

Secularism stands for scientific rationalism. It stresses logical thinking and abhors superstitions and irrational things. Realising this, our education today puts much emphasis on science teaching. At all levels of schooling science is taught in a practical manner that it might influence the attitudes and values of the pupils. The spirit of science with emphasis on enquiry, experimentation, proof and critical outlook, permeates the teaching of other subjects also.

4. *Teachers*

The teachers today are expected to treat their pupils in an impartial manner. They have to eschew all caste, community and class considerations in dealing with students and colleagues. Equal respect has to be given to all students and to all religious groups. Effort is made by every conscientious teacher to behave in a truly democratic and fair manner.

Thus our educational system is trying to create a social climate in the country in which secular values are sought to be promoted effectively and enthusiastically.

Limitations of Our Educational System in Promoting Secularism

Building up a secular state is a very challenging task, especially in a country like India in which traditional institutions like religion, caste, untouchability and dowry have been prevailing for thousands of years. Despite the best intensions of our constitution makers and truly great leaders climate of secularism in India. The main limitations of our educational system in this task are as follows:

1. *Traditional Bias and Narrow Outlook*

There are denominational schools functioning with a lot of freedom. There are D.A.V. schools, Jain Schools, Vaish Schools, Ahir Schools, Kayastha Pathshalas, Shia Schools, Catholic Schools, Rajput Schools etc. in which children of the respective communities or caste are admitted on preferational basis, and also teachers of the same communities are preferred. This practice is serious limitation in the functioning of Indian education as an integrative and secular force in our society.

Many of the Indian educational institutions at all levels suffer from the traditional bias of caste, community, sex and other factors. In matters of appointment of teachers, admission of students, giving scholarship and distributing favours and even awarding of marks in examinations, many of our educational administrators and teachers behave in prejudicial and irrational ways. In some state universities, teachers from other states are not allowed to seek appointments due to parochial or regional consideration. In denominational institutions employees of other communities suffer different kinds of discriminations and injustice. Despite all professed faith in secularism, in reality some of our educational administrators openly favour their caste and community members and have a deep-seated prejudice towards some others. This is why many of the educational institutions have been reduced to the level of houses of dirty politics, animosity and conflicts. Sometimes it is also seen that some of the teachers and students have deep-seated prejudice against pupils belonging to lower castes, minority community, tribal groups, rural backgrounds, lower social class etc. They illtreat them in a variety of ways.

2. *Too Much Emphasis on Theoretical Learning*

The educational curricula emphasised many things only in theory. Very little effort is made to change the values and attitudes of the students. It is a pity that many people with higher education do not hesitate to demand big dowries, are too much fastidious about *gotras* and sub-castes in deciding marriage, ill treat women folk and do not show respect to other religions. The lack of tolerance and courtesy on the part of the students and other towards villagers, women, poor people, minority community members, old people etc. in the buses, trains and other public places, reveals that the education has failed to change their value system in the desired manner.

3. *Neglect of Religious and Cultural Celebration*

It has been observed that on the days of important religious fairs, festivals and birthdays, schools and colleges observe holidays. Seldom are programmes conducted in institutions especially in higher institutions, on these days to highlight the best thoughts and values associated with them. The result is that the students do not get enough opportunities to advantage in inculcating desirable values and promoting secularism.

4. *Neglect of Group Activities*

Schools do not encourage many group activities. There is tendency on the part of teachers to neglect group activities and group methods of teaching and learning. This is a serious limitation in the promotion of secular and free ideas and values.

5. *Other Factors*

Some other factors that work against creating a secular atmosphere in the country are:

- Due to widespread illiteracy and want of adequate education, few people know the essence of their own religion or the religion they profess to follow.
- Economic and political functions in such a situation easily get projected into the religious sphere and lead to religious

fanaticism often exploited by political or other vested interests.

— Teachers by and large are ill-equipped to teach values and secular attitudes by example or by precept.

In institution like this where other educational institutional agencies such as the family, community and the mass media do not play an adequate role in the promotion of the desired value system, the role of schools invariably assumes great importance.

Secularism in Practice Today

As earlier mentioned the Indian Constitution gives the key importance to secularism in India. Later many commissions and policies also have put much stress on secularism to inculcate it in the citizens of India through education. Thereby the government has been trying to take different steps to achieve literacy and secularism together with national integration.

N.P.E. 1986 aimed at national integration, equal opportunity as well as the secularism and started Navodya schools. It has already come in practice. Within four years there have been quite a few Navodya schools in different states in India. These are residential schools where the students from different states, with different religion, and caste are taken. All the students live together, pray together, learn together and learn cooperation, unity, love and other human values. Students are selected from every state mainly from the rural area irrespective of their caste, creed or denomination.

Entry in the temples, churches and other religious places like pilgrimages is made free today. Any one from any religion whether high class or low class all have the equal right to enter into these places. A person in India is free to choose any religion and practice.

Inter-caste and inter-religion marriage is another practice in modern society in India. There have been many instances when these kinds of marriages are heard of and seen. Yet there is much scope in this issue to improve.

Schools, colleges, hostels and government offices, railways or in any office, anyone with eligibility can get employment irrespective of his caste, religion or denomination.

The question arises whether education has been able to achieve the goal of secularism.

Everyday new and our day-to-day life reveals that

communalism is deeply rooted in most of Indian citizens. We try to prove that our religion is good and other religions are not good. Religion can never be good or bad but the people practising those religions are at fault. There are many instances working against the goal of secularism. The issues of Punjab, Kashmir, Ram Janam Bhoomi, the enemity between Hindus and Muslims etc. These issues are the clear sign that the education today has not been able to achieve the goal of secularism. Today these political issues have affected every group in the society. All are suspicious about the other and man is not bothered for human life and kills others so brutally. A man is not really free to choose a religion of his own choice because of the other barriers that follow after this. He is excommunicated from the society which is the greatest punishment for man as social being. He is torchered in many ways.

When a person meets an unknown person in the offices especially during recruitment, in the train, bus—either he is asked or he himself asks about the caste, religion etc. He feels happy and comfortable with a person of his own group. This also shows that secularism has not been understood or they do not want to practice it.

The disparity among individuals or the different groups in the society regarding rights and equality in opportunity. Example:— the issue of reservation of seats in educational institutions or in the employment exchanges for ST/SC.

During the time of election the candidates want support from their own group and religion as well as caste become the main reason to support him without seeing whether he is worthy or not. People want majority of the representatives in the Parliament from their groups. This makes people blind to see the harm that is being done to other groups of the society. Today the election has become a communalism issue.

Likewise there are many examples to tell how secularism is being practised in India. It seems secularism has a place only in the Constitution, different commissions and policies and in practice it has very little place in the society.

However, the government is trying her best to bring secularism in the country through different ways as mentioned earlier. Inspite of all the critical issues man can hope for good, education therefore should have much more positive role than it has been so far in preparing people for a secular society.

References

1. Singh, Yogendra, *Sociological Foundations of Education*, Educational Publishers, Bombay, 1981.
2. Walia, J.S., *Principles and Methods of Education*, Paul Publishers, Jalandhar City, Punjab, 1980.
3. Johari, J.C., *Indian Government and Constitution*, Vishal Publications, Delhi, 1990, pp. 366, 394.
4. *Ibid.*, p. 395.
5. Aggarwal, R.N., *National Movement and Constitutional Development of India*, Vishal Publications, Delhi, 1973.
6. *Ibid.*, p. 245.
7. Safaya, R.N., *Current Problems in Indian Education*, Dhanpat Rai and Sons, Jallandhar, Punjab, 1970.
8. Education and National Development, *Report of the Education Commission*, 1964-66, NCERT, 1971.
9. *National Policy of Education*, Ministry of H.R.D. Government of India, New Delhi, 1986, p. 21.
10. "Towards an Enlightened and Humane Society," *Report of the Committee for Review of National Policy on Education*, New Delhi, 1990.
11. *Report of the National Commission on Teachers* (1983-85).
12. *Consulative Commission on Secondary Education*, England, 1939.
13. *Report of the University Education Commission* (1948-49) and Sri Prakas Committee on Religious and Moral Education, 1959.

8

Equity in Education

Concern for Inequities in Education

Concern for inequities in education stems not only from a moral commitment to the deprived but also from the viewpoint of nation building. Human resource development strategy calls for maturation and optimal utilisation of all segments of the population. Education has been rightly considered as an important input in such a development of human resources in the country. It was hoped that the phenomenal growth in educational facilities since Independence would lead to minimisation of inequities in this sector. It was, however, realised within a quarter century of independence that the expansion of educational facilities is not necessarily accompanied by equalisation of opportunities for all. It was noted that the expansion in education facilities are initially utilised by the advanced areas and advantaged sections of the society and as a consequence inter-regional/inter-group disparities tend to get accentuated in the first phase of development unless deliberate intervention in favour of the deprived is resorted to.

'Growth with equity' is now considered to be one of the objectives of planning in many of the developing countries. It may be noted that there is in the context of the developing countries, no contradiction between the demands for equity and growth. Equity without growth is a stagnant cesspool, wherein only misery, ignorance, obstantism and superstition can be equitably distributed. Growth without equity leads to the accentuation of structural disequilibrium and, chronic persistence of low purchasing power

of the mass of the toiling people constrains growth itself. The social concerns for the two can be handled together sustaining and sustained by each other.

It was in this context that equalisation of educational opportunities was recognised as one of the major goals of Indian educational policy. The National Policy Resolution, 1968, calls for strenuous efforts to correct regional imbalances and minimise inter-group disparities in the educational sphere. The National Policy on Education (1986) lays special emphasis on the removal of disparities and equalisation of educational opportunity by attending to the specific needs of those who have been denied equality so far.

Concept of Equity

The concept of equity can be understood by differentiating the two terms i.e., equality and equity. While the concept of 'equality' in general and 'equality of opportunity' in education in particular, have a long history, the concept of equity in education is a more recent one. There is, considerable confusion regarding the meaning of the two terms—equality and equity—and these have been used inter-changeably by scholars although literally they have a very different connotation. Bronfenbrenner (1973) distinguishes between these concepts by taking 'equity' to mean social justice, or fairness. It refers to a subjective and ethical judgement. 'Equality' refers to the pattern of distribution of something such as income or education. It is more objective and a descriptive term and can be measured. But equity, or fairness, of a situation of inequality can be evaluated only by appealing to value judgement.[1]

In education the idea of 'equality of opportunity' came in with French Revolution and took shape in United States of America after the war of American Independence. The concept of equality of opportunity in education started with provision for 'equal access'. Later on 'equal input' we considered necessary for equalising educational opportunities. Today, alongwith equal access and equal input, 'equal output' is considered a necessary criteria. The last one calls for measures of protective discrimination in favour of the disadvantaged sections of the society. Equity in education can also be achieved by pursuing the policy of protective discrimination in favour of the disadvantaged section of the society. In this sense, today equality and equity in education have the same connotation and most of the developing countries of the world have these as major goals of education policy.

Soon after attainment of independence in 1947, 'India also committed itself to achieve an egalitarian social order where equality in general and equality of opportunity in particular were taken as important elements of State Policy'. Further, under Article 46 of the Deirective Principles of state policy, the State was *directed* "to promote with special care the education and economic interests of the weaker sections of the society, and in particular of SC, ST and girls".[2]

Planned efforts have been made since independence to achieve growth of all parts of the country and all the groups of population. Special allocation for the backward areas and incentive and facilities for different groups of disadvantaged are all part of the strategy to achieve a more equitable distribution of opportunities.

The Need for Measurement

The situation of the backward regions and deprived groups has improved as a result of planned strategy but, it is not known if the disparities among different regions and groups have also decreased. In fact, the evidence in this regard is conflicting, depending on the variables chosen and statistics used. From view point of any meaningful policy for reduction of inequalities it is important to assess the reality objectively. For this purpose it is necessary to work out an index on the basis of commonly agreed indicators.

An indicator is a statistics which facilitates concise, comprehensive and balanced judgement about certain aspect of reality. It is a direct measure of welfare and as such if it changes in the right direction, it can be said that things have become better or people are better off. Indicators help in measuring both the qualitative as well as quantitative aspects of an objective reality. Quality reflects the identity of an object and as such cannot be brokenup into homogenous parts, the moment that is done identity is lost, consequently it can not be measured in itself. Quantity, on the other hand, is capable of being increased or decreased without changing its character. Hence one has to select quantitative indicaters of quality in order to make qualitative assessment.

For example to measure educational growth, which is one component of educational development, first of all one has to select the quantitative indicators such as,

(*i*) number of schools per 10,000 population,
(*ii*) literacy rates,
(*iii*) enrolment ratios at elementary level,
(*iv*) enrolment ratios in higher education,
(*v*) number of teachers at different levels,
(*vi*) growth in per pupil expenditure etc.

The values of these indicators either singly or after composition help in assessing the educational growth.

Prescription follows assessment of the situation. Here first of all one identifies the constraints to the growth and then proposes operational strategy. Once again the person moves from quality to quantity. Quality gives the direction to quantity while quantity gives accuracy precision and depth to quality. Both are necessary aspects of indicator construction.

This paper starts by highlighting the concern for equity and importance of indicators in assessment of reality. It proceeds to describe the inequities in Indian society and the basis of the same. It is followed by selection of educational parameters for assessment and then identifies relevant indicators for each of the parameters. The concluding part of the paper raises some methodological isssues in the measurement of inequities in education in India.

Inequities in the Indian Education

The Socio-economic Context

Inequity in education is not purely an educational issue for it cuts across the entire social, economic and political fabric of a nation. The social disparities that show up in educational systems are in no small extent, reflection on deeply embodied inequalities in the whole society and economy. In most of the countries the disparities are tied to sex, geographical location and socio-economic status. The available evidence shows that inspite of efforts at large scale expansion, the disparities still exist literally in all the countries. The forces underlying disparities are too complex to explain by a single theory of one way cause and effect.

Indian society is one of the most inegalitarian society, the basis of disparities being mainly caste, sex, ethnicity and place of residence. The caste inequalities are the most unique form of inequalities in Indian society and they draw their strength from ancient religious activities. The other forms of inequalities are common to all the countries though their magnitude differs from country to country. What makes the Indian situation most peculiar is the fact that there are layers and layers of disparities. Thus there are disparities between males and females, between people living in urban areas and, rural areas and between economically more advanced regions and less advanced regions. However the most deprived is the SC/ST female living in rural areas of a backward region. We shall return to this aspect in a separate section. At present we shall discuss the basis of inequalities in the Indian society and its manifestation in education.

Male-female Disparities

The most common form of disparities in the Indian and as in most of the pre-industrial societies is, male-female inequalities, wherin female was assigned a place in the home to bear children, look after her husband and otherwise to drudge for the household. Even here she had no hand in decision making.

Modernisation has done little to improve the status of women in Third World countries. The process of modernization in these societies has followed a return creating two way economy, one with capital intensive modern sector, and the other with labour intensive traditional sector.

Scheduled Caste and Non-scheduled Caste Disparities

In India, the exclusion of SC from education was supported by the educational theories of ancient and medieval times which were based on the assumption that those who work should not think and those who think should not work. A Brahmin should not touch the plough and a Shudra should not touch the Vedas. Contemplation was considered to be the only source of knowledge and this could be best achieved in the solitude of a Himalayan peak in the shade of a Banyan tree in the seclusion of jungle. This was not peculiar to India. Even in Plato's Republic, slaves were denied education.

The separation of work from knowledge was operationalised by the separation of training from education. The former was intended to transfer the skills of labour and secrets of craftmanship to the younger generation of toiling poor, the latter was intended to pass on the abstracted generalisation of social practice as gems of knowledge to the propertied class to enable them wield the power through knowledge and appropriate surpluses generated by the labour of the former. The separation of work from knowledge and work from power has been the most potent instrument of inequalisation.

In the Third World countries, however, Industrial Revolution was not allowed to take place and the socio-economic conditions, which had led to narrowing of the gap between work and education in the developed countries of the world in the wake of Industrial Revolution, were not allowed to emerge in the Third World countries. On the other hand, the educational system of the colonial countries tended to strengthen the separation of work from education.

In India, since Independence efforts have been made to break the dichotomy between work and education by introducing work eperience in school and by vocationalisation of the secondary education and professionalisation of higher education. Special incentives and facilities are also being provided to bring the traditionally working classes (SC) within the fold of educational system. There is some progress[3] but the situation continues to be largely unsatisfactory not only quantitatively but more so qualitatively.[4]

Scheduled Tribes, Non-scheduled Tribes Disparities

The Scheduled Tribes, in Indian constitutional terminology form yet another group of deprived in our country. As per 1981 Census they numbered 49.8 million (excluding Assam and Karnataka) constituting about 7.9 per cent of country's total population. Speaking about 105 languages they are mostly concentrated in the states of Orissa, Bihar, Madhya Pradesh, Andhra Pradesh, Maharashtra, Gujarat and Rajasthan where they account for about 80 per cent of total tribal population of the country. However, in none of these states they comprise more than 25 per cent of the total population of the state. In some of the north-eastern states on the other hand, they constitute more than 80 per cent of the population of the states though their combined number in these state is less than 4 millions.[5]

The tribals differ greatly in stage of their development[6] but they share certain common characteristics which mark them out as one of the most disadvantaged groups. In the first instance they occupy tracts of slopy land, hills and forests having been ousted from great fertile valleys. They are in command of poor resource regions. Secondly, the communication and infrastructure in the area is little developed which has led to the isolation of tribals from rest of the world as well as from one another.[7] Lack of cross-fertilisation of ideas has been responsible for hampered growth and advancement. The level of technology has remained low. The problems of tribals were further aggravated by the British who followed a policy of isolation. Thus the tribals were further removed from the mainstream. What is worse they were all the time exploited by the non-tribals who took advantage of their simplicity and innocence. Their produce was purchased at a very low price and they were alienated from land for non-payment of fictitious loans. In their own land they were treated as serfs for minor default. The physical isolation of tribals and the system of economic exploitation acted as a serious constraint to their educational development.[8]

In India, since Independence efforts have been made to make tribals part of national stream by introducing common political institutions in the areas, and by enrolling them in services as a matter of deliberate policy. Industries are also being set up in the tribal areas to provide for gainful employment to the tribals. Education has been considered as an important input in tribal developement and in the various Five Years Plans increasing allocations are being made for the welfare of the tribals in education. Number of special incentives and facilities have also been provided with a view to enable these groups to avail the educational facilities. As a result literacy rates of ST have improved from 8.3 per cent in 1961 to 16.3 per cent in 1981.[9] Enrolment have also increased at various levels of education. However, the gap between the ST and N.S.T. continues not only in literacy but also in enrolments. Drop-out rates continue to be higher and enrolment percentage of ST *vis-a-vis* NST at each successive level becomes lower and lower. In higher education the proportion in science stream and prestigious professional courses continue to be low. In services, their percentages are not commensurate to their population proportion.

The continued low untilisation of facilities by the tribals has been explained both in terms of external constraints—ecological, socio-economic and psychological, as well as internal constraints of the school system such as structure of school system, organisation, content and medium of instruction and methods of teaching.[10] By and large the spread of education among the tribals is contingent of the state of their social evolution, ecological setting, mode of economy, their exposure to language other than their own dialect, the pattern of economic interaction with non-tribal groups in the neighbourhood, the role of tribal elite and the exogenous forces that operated in the tribal region before and after independence.[11]

Rural-Urban Disparities

The rural urban disparities in education are part of a much broader imbalance in rural and urban economic and social development which underlines the heavy concentration of extreme poverty in rural areas of most of the developing countries. The major basis of differentiation between rural and urban areas is the radically different type of occupational structure of the two communities, where the occupation followed by the rural people are mostly agricultural, those pursued by people in the urban area are mostly non-agricultural. This results in selective migration to urban areas which brings about polarisation of rural urban people on a number of variables including that of education. Besides the selective migration the different type of facilities in two different kind of areas further accentuate the characteristics of their members.

Today educational structures, in most of the developing countries exhibit two educational systems: an urban system that is already close to universal primary schooling in many instance (except for slum children), and an impressive higher secondary and post-secondary enrolment as compared to 25 years ago, and a rural system typically composed of thinly spread (often incomplete) primary schools, with few, if any, secondary schools, and no higher education whatever above them. The practical effect of this is that the rural children who often comprise 70 to 90 per cent of total nation's children, have drastically smaller chances than their urban counterparts of entering the University. Ironically, even the agricultural colleges in many developing countries admit comparatively few people with rural background because their poor secondary preparation puts them at serious competitive disadvantage with mediocre urban secondary graduates who are not good enough to get into regular university and choose agricultural college as the last resort (often with no intention of entering a rural career).

In India also there are rural-urban disparities of high order, the rural literacy rates being only 29.57 per cent in 2001 as compared to urban literacy rates of 57.19 per cent. The provision of schooling facilities in rural and urban areas are widely different in terms of availability of schools within the habitation or within 1 km of walking distance. Disparities are larger in terms of infrastructural facilities and percentage of trained teachers which make urban schools qualitatively superior to the rural schools.[12]

Regional Disparities in Education

Yet another dimension of inequities in education is spatial/regional. This dimension embraces all the other forms of inequities. Regional disparities in education reflect on the physical aspect of accessibility and quantitative and qualitative aspect of utilisation. The educational disparities in this context are part of marked disparities in socio-economic conditions across the region[13] which help certain regions to acquire relatively greater importance than others and enable them to play a decisive role in the subsequent process of human capital formation. It is through these processes that a hierarchical and multi-level system of fields emerges through the nesting of sub-fields from the local, through the sub-regional and regional to the national level.

Regional disparities are common to all the countries[14] but these have diminished considerably in the developed countries since industrial revolution and more so since World War II. In developing countries, however, the situation is far worse. In these countries not only industrial revolution was not allowed to take place but the nature of colonial rule distorted the process of natural growth. Even the five decades of planning in India, backed by the system of incentives and special allocations for the deprived regions, has failed to initiate a process of balanced regional development. Not only have vertical disparities accentuated during the period, the horizontal balance too, showed signs of deterioration.[15] This has been partly due to settlement hierarchy inherited from colonial system wherein large cities with relatively high secondary and tertiary sectors acted as nodal points of development.

An important feature of regional disparities in India, as also in other third world countries, is high degree of temporal stability which is largely the composite effect of historical process, on the one hand, and of the current developmental strategies, on the other.[16]

Spatial disparities in India are found at variety of scales. For example, there are disparities between different states, between districts within the same state or region, between different blocks within a district. So far much of the work in regional disparities in India has taken 'state' as the unit of analysis. This may, however, hide more of differences than reveal.[17] For any meaningful analysis of regional disparities in the Indian context district needs to be taken as the unit of analysis. District as an administrative unit not only has a particular vitality in the Indian context but it is only at this level that remedial action for minimisation of regional disparitites can be effectively undertaken.

Pyramid of Inequality

As pointed out earlier, inequalities in education seldom express themselves singly as between two discrete categories. In fact, in a given societal set up, there are layers and layers of disparities. Taking the Indian situation specifically there are disparities between males and females, between rural areas and urban areas, between scheduled groups and non-scheduled groups, between advanced regions and backward regions of a state. Females have been found to be educationally deprived as compared to male but it is also observed that an urban female of non-scheduled group is less deprived as compared to a rural male or a scheduled caste male of urban area. She is certainly much better off as compared to females of any other category. To understand the system of inequalities in a realistic perspective it is necessary to know the relative deprivation of various groups in a society. This can be done by building a pyramid of inequalities.

In the Indian context one needs at least to consider the following sub-groups:

- *(i)* Males as compared to females.
- *(ii)* Rural males as compared to urban males.
- *(iii)* Rural people as compared to urban people.
- *(iv)* Rural females as compared to urban females.
- *(v)* SC males as compared to SC females.
- *(vi)* SC rural males as compared to SC rural females.
- *(vii)* SC urban males as compared to SC urban females.
- *(viii)* Rural SC as compared to urban SC.
- *(ix)* SC rural males as compared to SC urban males.
- *(x)* SC rural females as compared to SC urban females.
- *(xi)* ST males as compared to ST females.

(xii) ST rural males as compared to ST rural females.
(xiii) ST urban males as compared to ST urban females.
(xiv) Rural ST as compared to urban ST.
(xv) ST rural males as compared to ST urban males.
(xvi) ST rural females as compared to ST urban females.

Factors of Educational Inequities and Indicators

Educational inequities get expressed in a variety of forms. Starting from unequal access (availability of schooling facilities and their utilisation) it extends to unequal inputs (allocation of physical and material resources) and then to unequal outputs (completion rates, performance not only in terms of achievement scores but subsequent life chances). The indicator of equality have similarly been classified in three broad categories:

1. *Indicators of formal Equality of Access*—These include
   (i) enrolment ratios at all the levels and types of instruction by sex, race, I.Q. and class of origin.
   (ii) transition coefficients (including entry and exit) by sex, race, I.Q. and class of origin.
2. *Indicators of quality of Content*—This class of indicators cover
   (i) monetary resource input per child by sex, race, social class and region at all the levels of education,
   (ii) educational level of teachers,
   (iii) average social class origin of teachers,
   (iv) proportion of educational resources spent on special provision for groups seen as disadvantaged by the system.
3. *Indicators of Equality of Performance*—These comprise
   (i) achievement scores by race, sex, I. Q., social class at all levels,
   (ii) occupation and income by different educational levels of achievement controlling for race, age, social class, etc.[18]

The IIEP monograph on Regional Disparities has suggested a new scheme of indicators under two broad cateogories i.e.,

(i) Indicators of Means, and
(ii) Indicators of Results.[19]

These have been synoptically presented as follows:

	Indicators of Means	*Indicators of Results*
A.	Accessibility — physical — economic — socio-cultural	Access to the different levels of the educational system
B.	Formal quality of the educational service — Composition and qualification of the groups — composition and grouping of pupils — Availability and quality of facilities — Availability and quality of buildings	Progress through school — Promotion — Excess years in schools — Retention
C.	Actual quality of the Education Services — Degree of utilisation of facilities — Pedagogical attitudes of teachers — Social climate of the school	Level of Cognitive Achievements, Skills, Attitudes

Two indicators most commonly used in many of the international studies are 'Literacy Rates' and 'Enrolment Ratios' for different levels of education. On the basis of these two indicators the countries are classified either as educationally advanced or educationally backward. In the intra-country studies different scholars have made use of different indicators depending on the definition of equity and the availability of data. Here the most commonly used indicators are:

(i) availability of schooling facilities in different areas,

(ii) enrolment ratios for pupil classified by sex, region and socio-economic status,

(*iii*) retention rates of pupils classified by sex, ethnicity, region and socio-economic status,

(*iv*) achievement scores for pupils classified by sex, and place of residence.

Any attempt at construction of composite index of equity must take into account all the facts in which educational inequities express themselves. In a study conducted at NIEPA, a comprehensive scheme of classification of indicators has been worked out wherein objectives of the educational system and data availability has been a major consideration. The indicators have been classified in the following seven broad categories for the purpose of the study:

(*i*) Indicators of accessibility
(*ii*) Indicators of availability
(*iii*) Indicators of quantity
(*iv*) Indicators of quality
(*v*) Indicators of inter-connectivity
(*vi*) Indicators of equity
(*vii*) Indicators of utility

In all, more than 200 indicators have been identified in the above seven broad categories.

In what follows an attempt is made to take each of the class of indicators separately, see what they mean and then list the indicators under each of the categories.

(*i*) *Indicators of Accessibility*

Accessibility involves opening of schools in such a way that children enjoy equal opportunity of access to them. Generally accessibility is defined in terms of physical accessibility i.e., distance, relief, communication and time taken to travel between school and home, bearing in mind the available means of transport.

As the education system is arranged in the form of successive cycles, namely, primary, middle, secondary, and higher, which more often than not implies a change in school at each successive cycle, the problem of accessibility is to be considered separately for each level. It is, however, not possible that schools at all level could be offered in the same locality. In that case, equalisation of accessibility involves provision of different services aimed to reduce the time spent on school transport and frequency of journeys.

The vital indicators of accessibility are provision of school within defined walkable distance for each of the level of education, and existence of schooling facilities in each of the habitation. In the case of higher levels of availability of transport or provision for boarding facilities can be substituted for making the service accessible.

In addition to physical barriers to accessibility, there may be economic and socio-cultural barriers which mean that even if the schools are available within physical reach of the children, the poorer and socio-culturally deprived groups may not be able to make use of these facilities. The analysis of these kind of barriers may be particularly useful in the investigation of inter-group disparities within the same region. The measurement of economic accessibility may not be easy as it requires precise information on the cost of schooling (fee, private expenditure and opportunity cost). Socio-cultural accessibility is much more difficult to measure for it involves whole lot of questions regarding the culture of schools.[20]

(ii) Indicators of Availability

In the Indian context it is possible to measure only physical accessibility and the data availability makes possible the use of the following indicators only:

(i) Primary schools within the habitations for the total, SC/ ST habitation separately.

(ii) Primary schools within walking distance of 0.5 to 1 km. again separately for the total, SC and ST habitation. The same indicators with variation of distance can be computed for Middle Schools and High Schools.

(iii) Availability of schools per 10,000 population in the rural areas.

(iv) Availability of schools per 10,000 population in urban areas.

(iii) Indicators of Quantity

Given a certain organisational and spatial distribution of the school system, the next important question is how far the service is being used and what is the output of the system? The proportion of children utilising the service and those who are able to complete a given cycle, therefore, become quantitative indicators of the system.

Enrolment ratios at different levels and literacy rates are the two most commonly used indicators of quantity. This is because of the ready availability of data. Enrolment ratios is, however, a very global measure and combines the results of three phenomena, namely admission rates, repetition rates and dropout rates. In order to that this measure yields better results. It is necessary to have these indices separately.

In the context of inequalities in the Indian system these indicators will need to be worked out separately for rural and urban areas, males and females, scheduled castes and non-scheduled castes, scheduled tribes and non-scheduled tribes, economically advanced and economically backward districts.

The following indicators of quantity can be worked out for the different groups of people and for different levels of education:

- *(i)* Literacy Rates,
- *(ii)* Gross Enrolment Ratios,
- *(iii)* Net Enrolment Ratios,
- *(iv)* Admission Rates by Age in classes I, VI and IX,
- *(v)* Repetition Rates by Classes,
- *(vi)* Droup-out Rate for each Stage of Education.

(iv) Indicators of Quality

As said earlier, quality is very difficult to define. Its definition will, however, depend on the criterion used. Generally, quality is assessed on the basis of scholastic achievements. Unfortunately there is no conclusive research evidence to tell what service in school produces better results. Is it the physical facilities, the qualifications of teachers or the social climate of school? The choice of indicators will depend on the kind of answer. The problem is further complicated by the fact that there is, quite probably, phenomenon of the thresholds.

Equalisation of quality also poses difficult question. Should equalisation be conceived as a mere levelling process? Is it possible to lay similar standards throughout the country knowing well that situation differs greatly from one region to the other? And if diversity is to be respected, should we have minimum of standard as essential for quality?

Keeping the above in view one may think of several indicators of quality, such as quality of building, availability of equipment, number of pupils per teacher or number of pupil per class, social composition of pupil, qualification of teaching staff, etc.

These are the static indicators and provide for formal quality of service. This may be necessary condition, but for actual quality of service it may be necessary to know:

— the intensity and manner in which school infrastructure and facilities are being used,
— teachers' attitude and methods, and
— social climate prevailing in the school.

It may be difficult to measure quality thus defined but any interpretation of results should take this into account.

Bearing in mind the availability of the data in the Indian context the following indicators of quality can be worked out:

(i) Schools with *pucca* building in rural and urban areas separately,
(ii) Pupil-teacher ratios in Primary, Middle and Secondary Schools for rural/urban areas,
(iii) Teachers as percentage of sanctioned posts in primary, middle and secondary schools, separately for rural-urban areas,
(iv) Trained teachers as percentage of total teachers in Primary, Middle and Secondary Schools separately in rural and urban areas,
(v) Percentage of Primary, Middle and Secondary Schools having minimum equipment in rural/urban areas separately.

(v) Indicators of Inter-connectivity

Inter-connectivity in education refers to the unity of the educational process, where one stage of education is organically linked to next higher stage not only because the output of one becomes the input for the other, but also because development of one stage is essentially linked up with the development of other stage. For example it may not be possible to have good primary education without raising the quantity and quality of higher education since the latter provides teachers for the former. Similarly, it is not possible to have good higher education without a broad based and efficient system of elementary education. In a model situation of equity certain percentage of children should be able to move to next higher stage. Unfortunately there are no clear-cut norms to tell what percentage of primary school completers should go to middle schools or again what percentage of middle school completers should be transferred to secondary schools, and finally what percentage of school graduate should receive higher education. The ideal ratios will differ from country to country and within the same country over a period of time depending upon the absorptive capacity of the economy. For example, in a highly developed country the ratios of higher education enrolment to secondary school enrolment should be higher as compared to the less developed countries where the economy can maximally absorb middle level trained manpower.

(vi) Indicators of Equity

However within a country and from the view point of equity the norms should be same for each of the sub-groups. If the ratios of enrolment of different levels of education for the sub-groups within a country are different, then on equity consideration it should be a matter of concern.

Indicators of inter-connectivity from the view point of equity will, therefore, be based on the proportion of children at various levels of education to the relevant age groups for different sub-groups classified on the basis of residence or socio-economic status.

In the Indian context the relevant indicators of inter-connectivity can be spelled out as:

(i) Education pyramids separately for scheduled castes, scheduled tribes and non-scheduled groups.
(ii) Education pyramids separately for males and females.
(iii) Education pyramids separately for urban and rural areas.
(iv) Educational pyramids for different time periods for various sub-groups of the population.

(vii) Indicators of Utility

The debate over issues of equity would not have acquired the significance, but for the hope that education would serve to promote overall equality in the society. Human capital therorists see education as an important means of improving the stock of human capital. It is expected that education increases the marginal productivity of labour and as more people have chances to be educated more and more of them will improve their productivity. It is also suggested that disparities in income will also reduce as increased productivity brings increased income.

Although there is controversy regarding the role of education in narrowing the income inequalities, there is no dispute over the point that education improves the productivity of labour and more educated get higher income.

The relationship between education and productivity and, education and income, though fundamental is not direct and does not land itself to systematic analysis. It is, however, possible to work out the utility of education indirectly. One such method is to get the percentage. Strength of each educational stratum of workers in various occupational categories and multiply the same:

1. by the expected salary in accordance with the level of education and nature of jobs, and
2. the time period involved in each educational/vocational training.[21]

The underlying assumption is that the level of education by and large, determines the earnings of workers.

Considering the data availability and keeping the equity aspect in view it is possible to work out the following indicators of utility:

(i) Educational attainments (in terms of levels completed) for different groups of working population.

(ii) Distribution of total workers of different groups according to educational attainments and sector of economic activity.

(iii) Occupational distribution of different groups of people by their educational levels.

(iv) Income level of different groups of people by their education and occupation.

Methodological Issue in Indicator Construction

Several issues can be raised with respect to the measurement of inequities in education. The most important issue is when do we say that equity objective is achieved? The most ideal situation would be when disparities do not exist among different sub-groups on certain agreed criteria. In the Indian context where all the groups are far from the norm, the relevant issue would be: whether the sub-groups are moving in a manner that the disparities seem to get reduced, that is whether the system is better off at the present time in comparison to a reference data in the past?

There are several theoretical possibilities in which two groups which are being compared can move over time. These are:

(i) both the groups progress but deprived group progress faster and the two groups come nearer to each other.
(ii) both the groups progress in equal proportion so that the gap between them remains the same;
(iii) both the groups progress but the advanced group progresses faster and the gap widens;
(iv) Advanced group improves but deprived group remains static thus accentuating the disparities;
(v) deprived groups improves but the advanced group does not improve leading to the closure of the gap; and
(vi) both the groups are static and the gap continues.

In the Indian situation, the last three possibilities are not applicable. Moreover, because of the Government policy of positive discrimination in favour of the deprived groups, one expects that the deprived groups have progressed at a faster pace over the past 25-30 years, thus narrowing the gap between the advanced groups and the deprived ones.

A second issue relates to measurement of change. In measuring the change in the relative position of several groups over time, one can work out the gains by taking differences between the values of particular indicator at the present time and at some previous date and make a comparison in terms of the extent of improvement. One can also work out the extent of progress as the amount of relative change as percentage of the original level. Different methods of comparison of the groups give different results.

Thirdly, when two groups are compared over time, there are several ways in which they could be compared. In the educational fields, for example, as a crudest method, we may compare the changes in literacy rates alone. However, one may like to compare the progress at several levels, e.g., enrolment ratios at primary, middle, and secondary levels, retention rates, dropout rates, etc. Here the question is—How many and what type of indicators are essential and how can these be composited so that one arrives at an overall indicator which can enable the policy maker to say whether the inequities are reducing or widening? Some of the important questions in composition of an index are:

(a) Choice of component variables.
(b) Methods of combination.
(c) Weights to be assigned to each variable.

Further, there are two basic questions that need to be asked while measuring the degree of inequities:

(a) To what extent the quantity is being distributed equally among the sub-groups? The quantity in education are enrolment, finances, building, teachers, etc. For measuring them generally the teachnique of Lorenz curves or the Gini coefficient is used. However, in using the Gini coefficients there are certain problems. *Firstly* the Gini coefficients may turn out to be the same even though the curves may be of different shapes. It is believed that thiel index can bring out the variations more clearly. *Secondly,* although there may be improvement in different groups over time when do we say that equity objectives are being approached—is it when the lowest deciles are moving or when the higher deciles are moving. This may involve certain value judgement.

(b) Are the variations amongst individuals on a given characteristic of the same relative magnitude from one sub-group to another? Here the distribution of characteristic is not the focus, instead, it is the relative variation in each sub-group compared to the average level which is known to be different across the sub-groups. The teachnique of "co-efficient of variation" brings out clearly the inter-group comparisons rather than combinations. Typical quantities in an education system, which might be analysed with the coefficient of variation, are achievement test scores, financial outlays, and number of years of schoolings.

Finally, although there may be several indicators of equity which may be important in their own right, it becomes almost impossible to compute them if the relevant data are not available. In India, the disaggregation of educational statistics by sex, rural-urban residence, religion, scheduled castes, scheduled tribes, and non-scheduled groups, etc. for each unit of analysis—tehsils or districts—are not available to work out the various indicators at the desired level of disaggregation. One is constrained to use only those indicators which can be worked out from the available data. The population census provides certain indicators to measure educational progress but these become available once in ten years only. Collection of disaggregated data on a continuous basis will be necessary for development of relevant indicators for measurement of equity in education.

References

1. Bronfenbrenner, *Equity and Equality*, 1973.
2. Article 46 of the Directive Principles of State Policy.
3. Yogendra Singh, *The Process of Socialisation and Education*, papers in the Sociology in Education in India, NCERT, New Delhi, (ed.) 1967.
4. Persons, Talcott, *Social System*.
5. *Census*, 1981.
6. Gore, M.S. and others; papers in the *Sociology of Education in India* (eds.) NCERT, 1967, p. 142.
7. Mathur, S.S., *A Sociological Approach to Indian Education*, Vinod Pustak Mandir, Agra, 1973, p. 47.
8. Arora, G.S., *Tribe, Caste and Class*, Hyderabad, Administrative Staff College, p. 39.
9. *Censur Report*, 1981.
10. Arora, G.S., *Ibid*., p. 43.
11. The relative advancement of tribals of north-eastern region can be explained to the efforts of missionaries. The educational opportunities provided by the missionaries were quickly grabbed by all the sections of tribal communities. This was so because the tribal society, did not suffer from the inhibition characteristics of stratified societies.
12. The Fourth All India Survey conducted by the NCERT (1978).
13. Williamson's study of patterns of inequalities in West Germany validated the hypothesis that educational inequalities are deeply rooted in the social milieu and continue to constrain development even in developed countries.
14. Ryba examined territorial inequalities on a world scale by considering educational provision in relation to educational achievement. He showed that territorial inequalities may be noticed at every scale of analysis and that these have tended to persist over time.
15. See Kundu, A. and Raza, Moonis, *Indian Economy, A Regional Dimension*, 1982.

16. The study conducted by Raza and Aggarwal shows that inter-state disparities in literacy rates have continued to persist in spite of massive efforts. Also, the relative position of different states have not changed substantially specially in the case of state with low literacy rates.
17. It may be noted that districtwise disparities are much larger than state-wise disparities. Literacy rates, for example, vary from 7 per cent in East District of Arunachal Pradesh to 81 per cent in Kottayam district of Kerala and from 1.67 per cent for rural females in Jaisamler to over 79 per cent for the same group in Kottayam.
18. Organisation for Economic Cooperation and Development, Indicators of Performance of Educational System, OECD, Paris, 1973.
19. International Institute of Educational Planning, Reduction of Regional Disparities: *The Role of Educational Planning,* UNESCO, Paris, 1981.
20. Carron, Gabriel and Chau, Ta Ngoc, Reduction Disparities. *The Role of Educational Planning,* IJEP, Paris, 1981, p. 62.
21. See Akhtar Hussain, *Educational Structure of Working Labour Force in India, 1961. Regional Analysis* unpublished M.Phil. dissertation, JNU, 1975.

9

Universal Literacy

"Education has a acculturing role. It refines sensitivities and perceptions that contribute to national cohesion a scientific spirit. . . . . . . thus furthering the goals of socialism, secularism and democracy enshrined in the constitution." 2.2 - *N.P.E. 1986.*[1]

India is the largest democracy of the world for being a democratic country, there is a prerequisite, that people choose a right candidate who can decide their future. India, which is called fourth world country (Alpha), it becomes a necessity to develop our country, in which we live. The country can develop provided the potentials of its people are properly used (not exploited) in building the nation, and perhaps education can play a vital role. Education in itself has got potentials to develop in its recepients certain qualities to serve their own basic needs.

> "Literacy is an important means of meeting an individual's basic needs of acquiring knowledge pertinent to changes in existing practices and skills, it helps to be able to use the services provided. It is also observed that literacy is a critical factor in enhancing the benefits derived from interventions designed to improve the quality of life of people." *Malhotra*, 1992.[2]
>
> "Spreading literacy has been an important programme since independence. Between 1951 to 1981 percentage of literacy spread from 16.67 per cent to 36.27 per cent. Illiterates have

> increased from 300 million to 437 million. Women comprise 57 per cent of illiterate population".[3] — *P O A 1985.*

In order to fulfill the goals enshrined in the Constitution to provide free, compulsory, elementary education. It is a must to make education more appealing to all irrespective of all castes, creed and sex. Education can be made responsive only if it caters to social demands.

In order to make education to cater to the social demands, it has to be planned at a micro level, keeping in view the social psychological needs and the need hierarchy of Abraham Maslaw i.e. 5 stages physiological needs, security needs, belonging needs, self esteem and self actualization. Micro level planning will see to the local dialect, local examples and illustrations. Locally available material can be used in the teaching-learning process including the locally available teachers. The teachers in local areas can form their own curriculum, which will operate at the micro level.

Universal Literacy and Literacy Rates

Education is a sub-system of the social system. It draws all its resources from the society. As a matter of fact society has levied the task of teaching-learning upon educational sub-system. Education draws, content, pupils, teachers, finance and other material resources from the society so as to a certain extent education is taking the responsibility to acculture its pupils into the changing trends.

> "The Nation as a whole will assume the responsibility of providing resource support for implementing programme of education, transformation, reducing desparities, universalization of elementary education, adult literacy, scientific and technological research etc."[4] —*3.10. N.P.E. 1986.*

Education has its own history and as it is in the hands or is governed by the political sub-system. It is shaped accordingly. Education has taken up a enormously difficult task of carrying the burdens of past and showing the path of future and probably earlier task of carrying past makes it a slow process towards change.

Education on the one hand has to give qualitative aspect that is drawing out best in the man's mind, body and soul and on the other hand, it has the responsibility of giving qualitative education so that it can take in its purview elementary as well as adult education and provide education to all from the age of 6-35.

Literacy Rates—States and Union Territories

S.No.	*States*	*Literacy Rate 1991 Census in %*	*All India Ranking*
1.	Andhra Pradesh	45.11	25
2.	Assam	53.42	22
3.	Arunachal Pradesh	41.22	28
4.	Bihar	38.54	31
5.	Goa	76.96	5
6.	Gujarat	60.91	15
7.	Haryana	55.33	21
8.	Himachal Pradesh	63.54	11
9.	Jammu & Kashmir	26.67	32
10.	Karnataka	55.98	20
11.	Kerala	90.59	1
12.	Madhya Pradesh	43.45	26
13.	Maharashtra	63.05	12
14.	Manipur	60.96	14
15.	Meghalaya	48.26	24
16.	Mizoram	81.23	2
17.	Nagaland	61.30	13
18.	Orissa	48.55	23
19.	Punjab	57.14	18
20.	Rajasthan	38.81	30
21.	Sikkim	56.53	19
22.	Tamilnadu	63.72	10
23.	Tripura	60.39	16
24.	Uttar Pradesh	41.71	27
25.	West Bengal	57.72	17
Union Territories			
1.	Andaman & Nicobar	73.74	8
2.	Chandigarh	78.73	4
3.	Dadra and Nagar Haveli	39.45	29
4.	Delhi	76.09	6
5.	Daman and Diu	73.58	9
6.	Lakshadweep	79.23	3
7.	Pondichery	74.91	7
*	**All India**	**52.11**	

Note: Delhi has now been given the status of state. But when survey was done it was a Union Territory.[5]

> "Our ancient Scriptures define education as that which liberates that provides the instruments for liberation from ignorance and oppression. In the modern world, it would naturally include the ability to read and write, since that is the main instrument of learning. Hence the crucial importance of adult education, including adult literacy".[6] —*N.P.E. 1984. 4.10.*

Education on one hand has to give qualitative aspect that is drawing out best. It also has to cater to provide quantitative education to make it more reacheable to the masses. Universal literacy, has been in our plans since 1951. But it always remained a noble dream in the minds of educators and educationist. It could never become reality without the involvement of masses.

As it is evident from the above table Jammu & Kashmir has the lowest rate of literacy and Kerala has the highest. India still faces surmountable illiteracy rate of 47 per cent and for progress in socio-economic level, it needs to be eradicated.

As is evident from some researches the problem of universal literacy continues to be an impediment in the progress of our country, is because of following reasons:

1. Lack of interest in the content.
2. Busy in economic activities.
3. Poor facilities available.
4. Inadequate teachers.
5. Formal structure and its rigidness etc.

Problem in the Programme

1. Lack of Interest in Content

Content is not suitable to the students. They find it to be irrelevant and unpractical. The unsuitability is probably because they are unable to co-relate the content with their immediate environment.

2. Busy in Economic Activities

Some children in the early childhood have to do a lot of work to attain daily bread and for them education becomes a luxury, an unaforadable task. By unaffordable I don't mean financially but a time consuming task.

3. Poor Facilities Available

In some of the areas facilities are not available. Black Board, class room and chalks are also not available. The class room or the place wherever the literacy mission is carried out should be able to attract the children and adults to stay there and not to scare them.

4. *Inadequate Teachers*

In some remote rural areas and also in urban areas getting an appropriate teacher from the quota of SC and ST or even general at times is a difficult task. Inadequate teachers will include both untrained, undertrained and inadequate number.

5. *Formal Structure and its Rigidness*

Formal structure and its rigidness was a problem sometimes back, but it no more exist because the non-formal education has come to its rescue.

Today schools are available in the 2 kms area of village, mid-day meal and scholarship are also available in many states. The provision of taking teachers and trainee teachers from various areas of interest has been made. *(Acc. to Edu. Comm. Report N.P.E. 1986).*[7]

What we need is? or The need of hour is?

The critical development issue today is the continuous upgradation of skills so as to produce manpower resources of the kind and the number required by the society. Since participation by beneficiaries in the development programme is of crucial importance, systematic programme of adult education linked with national goals such as alleviation of poverty, national integration, environmental conservation, energisation of the cultural creativity of the people, observation of small family norm, promotion of women's equality etc. will be organised and the existing programme reviewed and strengthened.[8]

The whole nation must pledge itself to the eradication of illiteracy, particularly in the 15-35 age group. The Central and state governments, political parties and their mass organisations, the mass media and educational institutions must commit themselves to mass literacy programme of diverse. It will also have to involve on a large scale teachers, students, youth, voluntary agencies, employees concerted efforts will be made to harness various research agency to improve the pedagogical aspects of adult literacy. The mass literacy programme would include, in addition to literacy, functional knowledge and skills and also awareness among learners about the socio-economic reality and the possibility to change it.

The two points 4.11 and 4.12 of N.P.E. 1986 are of the view and want the nation to develop and continuously upgrade itself and this it says is possible only through mass literacy programmes which would include literacy functional knowledge and skills and also awareness among learners about the social and economic reality and to see to the possiblity of changing it.

Mass literacy programme should be taken as a pledge by all the countrymen, teachers, students, youth, voluntary agencies, research agencies, different employers and employees. Education in India stands at the cross roads today. Neither normal linear expansion nor existing pace and nature of improvement can meet the needs of the situation.

So what need to be done is to make education responsive to social demands:[9]

1. Make use of local community school.
2. Make use of neighbourhood school.
3. Renovate the curriculum.
4. Make text more attractive.
5. Mobilise the youth to take charge of educating.
6. Educate through street dramas.
7. Illustrate the success of people of their type as a result of education to motivate them.
8. Provide various incentives and facilities.
9. Give more of skill based and relevant education.
10. Provide for flescitime and need based schools.
11. Provide education through Technology.
12. Let voluntary organisation, social organisation and non-govt. organisation to take over the charge of education (mass).

Universal literacy can be achieved in my view if more of decentralization be given to curriculum development. If the curriculum is more appealing and the text-books if they become more odourful and have e.g.'s from their near vicinity more people can be attracted. Prior to the curriculum development, there is a need to bring about awareness amongst people that education is a strong instrument which can change their lives and make their mobility more easier. This kind of awareness is the best way to fix in their mind that education will really make all the difference and they can also become milestones in the progress of our country.

For bringing about this awareness a large number of students will have to be mobilised to bear the responsibility to make people aware about the benefits of education. And perhaps, if the students are successful in stirring the stagnant water of illiteracy even by the spell of words the flow of litereracy can sprout and soon take a stature of an ocean.

If somehow the need of education can be created in the mind of people, they themselves will find out ways and means of getting themselves educated. Some voluntary organisations will have to come forward for guiding the awakened people. The voluntary organisations can guide people as to from which source they can get education.

Some technical institutions may come to the rescue to giving some skill based training to our population. Educational technology can plan for a number of mobile van and provide ½ an hour programme in an area within a radius of 80 kms. or so for this purpose van's can be hired and donations can be collected from the local people (rich). The far off ideas and more of abstract terms can be explained more explicitly through the educational technology. Some help can be taken from government for acquiring funds in order to complete the programme successfully. Each person involved in the particular task will have to be made accountable hundred per cent.[10]

Now on curriculum development side. The curriculum should be planned at micro level that is at local level keeping in view the social demands:[11]

1. *Local Community School:* My local community school means the traditional mode of transferring culture that is practised in a particular community needs to be revived and revitalized. This may turn out to be effective.

2. *Neighbourhood School*: By neighbourhood schools I mean in a simple house a household wife can take the charge of educating the students living in neighbourhood. This can prove to be a positive propaganda, for a mass literacy programme.

3. *Renovation of Curriculum*: Though an expensive task, but will prove to be a leaping stride in attaining mass literacy by making it more relevant and close to immediate surroundings. From cover page itself it should be very attractive and appealing to students plus they should be cheap.

4. *Text-books More Attractive*: Text-books should be made more attractive in order to sustain interest of students. The texts should have enough space, colourful photographs, a neat print and top most will be understandable vernacular language.

5. *Mobilise Youth to take Charge of Educating*: Programme of action indicates a programme for students as each one teach one. That students should take responsibility of atleast making one person literate.

6. *Education Through Street Drama*: This is something that late Safdar Hashmi, used to practice educating through street drama. A few people can collect and on a script necessarily educational can perform street drama. It can be both in urban and also in rural areas.

7. *Illustrate the Success of People of their Type as a Result of Education to Motivate Them:* This can be possible either through Television network programme or through street drama. There is one programme on T. V. face in the crowd can make a reasonable success.

8. *Provide Various Incentives and Facilities*: Incentives in the form of mid-day meals and scholarship could not work. But perhaps more attractive school with proper facilities, school buildings and black boards etc. should be provided to attain this goal.

9. *Give More of Skill Based Education:* Skill based education will help those students who do a job, so that they can achieve a better say. The skills will help in generating the much needed money for bread and butter and may attract more number of people.

10. *Flexitime and Need Based Schools:* Though the idea is a bit foreign, but it can work in India. Whatever the student wants to learn according to his need and time adjustment can go and get education of the needed type. Suppose one is interested in learning motor mechanics. The time for it is 10 o'clock he can go at 10 and perhaps after 40 minutes of class he can go back to work. And at 10.40 there can be another class of making furniture i.e., carpentry so on and so forth.

11. *Education Through Technology:* It can be provided through TV's and Video's or through Tape Recorders, Grammophones short and abstract but local programme can be concertised. As indicated on next page of having a common set and a mobile van on hire in a area of 30 kms. for ½ an hour programmes. Donations can be collected for the purpose.

12. *Voluntary and Social Organisations:* This is the oldest way that has been pursued since years, and is potential enough to draw more number of students. Non-governmental organisations can also take on the charge of mass education.

The difficulty in making education respond to social demand.

Here one thought comes to my mind. Can education—a crucial instrument of development be given in the hands of people as to mould the way they like. And is it really possible?

The development of curriculum becomes an extremely difficult task. Because in country like ours where the dialect of a language are not even common in two villages and due to multi-linguistic pattern making books in each and every language is extremely difficult due to the cost involved in such an enormous task.

Plus availability of competent people from such an area is also a difficult task at times. The demands of society are there and these demands vary from person to person, area to area, region to region and state to state, so there are chances of getting lost. And perhaps if an average consensus is made we may find a way and reach to the existing situation.

Society is not consistent, it is very dynamic and it keeps on changing. In that case the education on lines of social demand and its goals will become flimsy and unreal.

Conclusion

According to Kothari Commission Destiny of India is shaped in class room. But if the rate of illiteracy remains to be same and its classes remain half filled, what will happen to its destiny?

> "The lack of a certain level of literacy inevitably leads to a deprivation of basic needs and a serious undermining of the potential for not only individual fulfilment but also National Development" *Malhotra* 1989.[12]

So, it becomes more necessary to develop literacy among the people in order to increase National Development. Attaining universal literacy is not an impossible task. It can be attained by various ways.

The inheritable problem that it has in it is development of curriculum with regards to social demands which varies from person to person and region to region which was also evidentially observed in the 'CAPE' project of 'UNICEF' framing curriculum in accordance to social needs is a real difficult task, but of course it is not an impossible task. It may be that keeping in view the quantitative education, the requisite quality will have to be dropped as we may be also dealing with first generation learners, and in some places with partially literate people.

References

1. *New Education Policy*, 1986.
2. Chaube, S. P., *Philosophical and Sociological Foundation of Education*, Vinod Pustak Mandir, Agra, 1981.
3. *Programme of Action*, 1985.
4. *New Education Policy*, 1986, 3.10.
5. *Census Report*, 1991.
6. *NPE*, 1986.
7. Jalaluddin, A.K., *Developmental Imperatives for Universalisation of Basic Education*, published in school education in the 1990s, pp. 28 to 44.
8. Lakshmi, T.K.S., and Yadav, M.S., Education—Its Evolving Characteristics published in New Frontiers of Education, Oct.-Dec. 1992, pp. 595-609.
9. Mohanty, Jagannath, *Modern Trends in Indian Education*, Deep and Deep Publication, New Delhi, 1988.
10. Shukla, Suresh Chandra, and Kumar, Krishna, *Sociological Perspective in Education*, Chanakya Publication, New Delhi, 1985.
11. Tyagi, P.N., *Education for All, A Graphic Presentation*, NIEPA 17-B, Shri Aurobindo Marg, New Delhi, p. 23.
12. Malhotra, P.L., *Education for All*, UNESCO Principal Office, Bangkok, Thailand, No. 30, Dec., 1989, p. 127.

10

Women Education in the Rural Set-Up

Any nation's march towards progress and prosperity will remain a dream, it's aspiration unrealised till the women mactively participate in all the developmental activities and therefore today education has a tremendous task to cope with. Four centuries ago Martin Luther King protested, "If every year, so much money is spent on buying machines of war why should not much more be provided to the active and intelligent women-folk who are capable of teaching and bringing up our young people".[1]

If we take in the Indian context, as Gandhiji said, "India is to be found in the villages, and it's in the villages, where education of the future generation should begin." Gandhi believed that, "It was from the lips and laps of the women that the next generation would be educated".[2] The importance of education needs to be emphasised for even as a housewife, she can assist in the development of the family and the nation. In the National Policy of Education, removal of illiteracy and retention was given top priority.[3] The Education was made compulsory till the age of 14, but in the year 1963 at a meeting of National Council for Women Education, a suggestion was made by the Union Education Minister that a committee be appointed with Shri M. Bhaktavatsalam as its chairman.

The Committee was specially appointed to look into the rural areas, wherein they (committee) were convinced that only through a willing and educated and informed public, any progress can be made and for that the official and involuntary agencies must come forward. There was also a need for a systematic and sustained programme which mobilised this effort.[4]

Fields for Co-operation of Public

Direct co-operation of the public should be encouraged in the following fields[5]

1. Establishing Private Schools.
2. Putting up school buildings.
3. Contributing voluntary labour for construction of schools.
4. Helping in the maintenance of school building.
5. Helping in providing suitable accommodation for teachers and students particularly in the rural areas.
6. Popularising education at primary level.
7. Undertaking necessary propaganda to make the profession of teaching for women popular.
8. Creating public opinions in favour of the teaching profession.
9. Encouraging married women to take-up studying.
10. Initiating action and participating in educative propaganda to breakdown traditional prejudices against girl's education.
11. Setting up and organising school betterment committees.
12. Supplying mid-day meals.
13. Supplying uniforms to poor and needy children.
14. Supplying free text-books and writing material to needy children.

The states' Council for Women's Education are the most suitable agencies for providing the organisation and leadership for mobilising community effort. And these voluntary agencies should help educate public opinion to promote girl's education as their main and primary responsibility.

State's Responsibility

The state's steps to forward girl's education in the rural areas:

1. School Improvement Conference.
2. Seminars.

3. Radio talks, audio-visual and distribution of informative pamphlets and brochures.
4. Enrolment drives, generally in June and special additional drives for girls education during Dussehra.
5. Assisting voluntary, welfare and other organisations, private individuals and other committees engaged in the field of rural development.

Popularisation of Girl's Education

1. *School Improvement Conferences:* They should be arranged in every village and town in order to bring about an educational awakening and advancement.
2. *Schools in All Areas:* The Centre/state should provide necessary schooling facilities in all areas and inhabitations, so that the rural population (300) can make use of them. The primary school should be within the radius of one mile.
3. *Pre-primary Schools:* It is important that these schools be attached to primary schools, so that the children are accustomed to schooling even at a tender age.
4. *More Attractive School Work:* School work should be more attractive and practical so that it helps them.
5. *Appointment of Women Teachers:* The women by general consent are considered to be the best at the primary stage, some attractive remuneration should be provided to the teachers working in the rural areas.
6. *Preference to Women in Rural Areas in Admission:* During selection of trainees for training schools and colleges special preference is to be given to women from rural areas seeking admission.
7. *Improvement in Inspection:* The inspecting staff should be adequate and strong if improvement is to be secured and waste reduced. A separate women inspectorate will help to bring in more girls to schools.
8. *More Central Bodies Assistance:* A study of the conditions prevailing in the rural areas where increasing the enrolment of girls in particular school be tackled in an organised and co-ordinated manner.
9. *Adult Education:* In the field of social education, a determined effort should be made to increase the number

of literacy classes for women in rural areas to carry out compaigns for the spread of literacy among the rural women.

10. *More Responisbility on the Local Bodies:* They should be made responsible for the availability of school building, equipment and the observance of the educational code in the state.
11. *Stages of Central Assistance:*

    (a) At Elementary stage:

    (i) Preparation and employment of women teachers.
    (ii) Grant of free books, writing materials and clothing to girls.
    (iii) Twin quarters for women teachers.

    (b) At Secondary stage:

    (i) Provision for separate schools for girls.
    (ii) Hostels.
    (iii) Grant of free books, writing materials and clothing to girls.
    (iv) Preparation and appointment of teachers in increasing numbers.

12. *School Building:* The provision of suitable school buildings is an urgent need for which cent percent central assistance or long-term central loan should be provided.
13. *Free Education:* The State should find ways and means of providing funds in order to make education free for all girls up to the secondary level. Unless this incentive is given, it will be very difficult for the parents in their present economic circumstances to afford girls education.
14. *State Council's for Women's Education:* The state Councils for Women's Education should strengthen the agencies by providing for them a proper secretariat and a suitable financial assistance to meet the expenses of TA and DA of the members, so that they are always in constant touch with the workers in the field thus providing, guidance and needed changes.
15. *Curriculum:* While the curriculum can be made same for both boys and girls at the primary and middle stages provision should be made for offering of electives

comprising subjects which would be of special interest to girls and which would help them later in the field of activity. The National and State Council in the "Differentiation of Curricula for boys and girls" should be carefully studied and action taken by the states to implement them as far as possible.

16. *Double Shifts:* In rural schools, where there is lack of accommodation and rush for admission, the double-shift is a temporary measure.
17. *Flexibility of School Hours:* Changing of school and school holidays to seasonal requirements. It suitable changes of hours of schooling will have to be considered in the backward and hilly areas, where due to climate, economic and other conditions, parents will not be in a position to send children to school while in fact, they could be employed on the farms during harvesting season. This is a temporary measure, till things improve and till the parents and guardians are educated so as to understand the need for proper schooling for girls.
18. *Extra labour by less Advanced states:* The states less advanced like Bihar, Jammu and Kashmir, Madhya Pradesh, Rajasthan, Uttar Pradesh could make extra efforts and should aim at additional enrolments in classes I to V and VI to VIII. At the secondary stage, the enrolment should nearly be doubled up, for ensuring that there is an adequate supply of women teachers.

The Education Commission fully endorsed the recommendations of the three committees which have examined the problem of (rural) women's education in recent years:

(i) The National committee on the Education of Women under Shrimati Durgabai Deshmukh.
(ii) Committee on Differentiation of curricula between boys and girls under Shrimati Hansa Mehta.
(iii) The committee under Shri M. Bhaktavatsalam which studied the problem in six states where women education is less developed.

It's then that the Commission observed:
"In the modern world, the role of women goes much beyond the home and the bringing up of children. She

> has to now adapt a career of her own and sharing equally with man the responsibility for the development of society in all aspects. This equal partnership will have to continue in the fight against hunger, poverty, ignorance and ill-health."[6]

Despite so many steps introduced the women education in the villages, our Committees and Commission do admit that there has been a delay in our progress mainly because of the slow progress of education among girls. There has been a wide discrepancy in the enrolment of boys and girls giving way to wastage and stagnation. The factors responsible for this slow growth may be accounted to the following. In a research conducted by the Commission it was found that in a village of Rajasthan, the girls school which had been opened remained sadly empty. One asks the question why this grim scenerio, for if boys are the men of future girls are the women. And right from the beginning the son is out and the girl stays indoor thereby confirming to her future role as a women. And for going to school one must go out. Psychologically speaking means exposure, acquiring of independence. Therefore, when the school is at a distance away in the rural areas, the distance between schools become greater for sisters than for brothers.

Secondly, the more illiteracy is there among mothers, the less chance their daughters have of receiving education. In a research conducted in U.P. only 35% schools had pre-primary enrolment.[7] This shows the lack of education leads to hindering growth of the present generations and specially in the case of girls, they seem to be less convinced by the uneradicable tradition that a daughter must help her mother.

Caught between the school and the home, girls who have the good fortune to go to school find it very difficult to complete their primary schooling. In rural areas, household duties is a crashing burden, wherein the girls are expected to work in the fields or are employed in cottage industries. Can we call their parents monsters "who sacrifice their daughters," certainly not. For they feel that such training is essential to them, for after all they are preparing their daughters for their future roles as mothers and wives.[8] The girls are often overwhelmed by this two-fold attitudes-our a stay down and therefore exhausted physically, they give less attention to studies. This drain on their physical energy cannot be ignored, especially when their bodies are already weakened.

Thirdly, the economic aspect, wherein to send the children to school, even when it's free, means an addition of extra burden to the family budget and the absence of the children who are at school means a prolonged loss of income. Parents withdraw their daughters in the first place and send their sons which contribute to the wastage of the National funds.

Fourthly, in point of fact, the syllabuses in the lower primary classes are generally identical for both sexes. Later the similarity ceases, for e.g. needle work is especially reserved for girls, and metal work for boys. Thus girls receive literary and artistic education, while boys are trained for technical subjects and in sports. In short, the principle that woman is made for the home and for keeping the traditions alive, man is made for going out into the world for progress. Thus, girls loose their opportunity to play their part in the re-shaping of the nation.

Next is the obstacle of marriage where in certain states they are married at a very young age. Though the Government has raised the age for marriage, then the problem persists and secondly, the girls of the age of 15 to 17 leave schools to get married, thus only adding to the present condition of wastage, thus going in acydic process, wherein economic pressures will stagnate their studies, thus the drop-outs keep on increasing every year.

It's not merely the economic factor, but also connected with the actual content of education, which often leads nowhere but to the University. Girls are not provided vocational courses for e.g. girls studying at teacher training colleges, at technical courses know they are getting for a specific occupation, thus bringing down the drop out rate.

Thus vocational guidance is often lacking. This state of affairs has a more adverse effect on the future of girls, who are restricted by tradition.

These are some of the major factors which contribute to the slow pace of villages, a necessity to bring the womenfolk into the main stream of life, which is only possible through an awareness among them. For spreading this awareness, it becomes a moral responsibility of every Indian educationist, to propagate it.

References

1. Bagal, Jogesh Chandra, *Women's Education in India*, New Delhi, 1902-21.
2. *Ibid.*, p. 131.
3. *NPE*, 1986.
4. "Report of the Education Commission", Ministry of Education, 1964-66.
5. Shrinivas, M.N., *Some Reflections on Dowry*, Oxford University Press, New Delhi, 1984.
6. Dasai, Chitra, *Girls' Education and Social Change*, A.R. Sheth and Co., 133, Princess Street Bombay, 1976.
7. Mathur, Y.B., *Women's Education in India*, University of Delhi, 1973.
8. Sharma, S.R., *Women's Education and Social Development*, Kanishka Publishing House, Kailash Nagar, Delhi, 1992.

11

Politicisation of Education

It is a common view that in a modern and rapidly changing society, it is necessary to divert significant portion of resources for education as today the education is considered an industry. The input and output factors are clearly spelled out and the entire system between these two aspects is so organised to yield the maximum output. As it is an organisation, so there must be some power distribution and closely related to power in politics. Politics relates to ways people gain and use power. A formal definition of politics according to Ashwathappa, "refers to those behaviours or activities that are not required as part of formal role in the organisation, but that influence, or attempt to influence, the distribution of advantages and disadvantages within the organisation." Again in the words of Bachorch and Lawles (1980), "Politics in organisation is the tacticle use of power to retain or obtain control of real or symbolic resources."[1] A political model of organisation that emphasises the power and conflict dynamics of conditions within the framework of bargaining relationship and bargaining tactics. In the words of Allen and Maya (1977), "Politics is the management of influence to obtain ends not sanctioned by the organisation or to obtain sanctioned ends through non sanctioned influence means."[2]

The political actions of educational institutions, administrators, board members as well as the action of parents, teachers are related directly and indirectly to hiring, retention, promotion, decisions, regarding institutions working from the teachers perspectives the motivation for engaging in practices associated with favouratism, common to most of groups included control, conflict, avoidance of embarrassment, responding to the expectation of others with status, power, friends, relatives and concern about public image.

Today education became a matter of primary concern to the state not only because educated citizens could provide better manpower but also it leads to National Integration. Education today is seen as the best available means to civilize and to rule the industrial classes has increasing been conceptualised on a sector act as a fillip to economic growth and in this sense it is an important area of investment. But in India in the case of limited resources and intense public competition, the idea that school and higher education is a social right to be provided, so the demand for education has preceded and out-paced rather than followed an lagged behind the ability of the economy to generate resource to meet this demand. So the concurrent growth of demand for school and higher education, the use of public authority and resources to meet most of these demands and the considerable influence of politics on education multiplied the points of interaction between the political and educational system and make the system politicise.

Politicisation

Politicisation involves the appropriation of educational structure, resources and the displacement of educational goals, organised by the politicians and community. The effect of politicisation is to attempt the educational goals and process of particular educational institutions to those of organised eradicational interests.

The politicisation of educational institutions is a part of larger process of politicisation in India which in increasing number of actors in various political attempt to maximise political resources and through them political influence and power. Educational institutions, particularly higher educational institutions, private or public need political influence to pursue their goals and to protect and enhance their interest and independence. They line in particular political and social environment from which they require sympathetic understanding without political influence, they cannot command the resources and the autonomy essential for their intellectual and material well-being. Politicisation in the context of relationship between the education and political system refers to the use of political skills, influence and strategies to ensure public decisions and allocations that are favourable to education generally to the needs and interests of particular institution.

The word politics has on the whole negative connotation in India. This connotation is indiscriminating and ill informed. There is misuse of politics. Politicisation in the management of public relations so as to gain advantages for oneself or for ones party. The working of such manipulation in that they are brought about through influence and that their results too frequently work injustice because they are planned for such immediate and shallow ends. In some quarters this study's attempts to keep the schools away from politics is viewed as great misfortunate. It is unthinkable that the institutions should be outside the political sphere since the school or institutions train the future citizens.

Discipline and Politics

The falling standard of education, indiscipline among students, teachers, workers in educational institutions are the general concern of the people who have any interest in education in any capacity. However, it is generally agreed that politics among teachers as well as students has contributed significantly for this state of affairs i.e. politicisation as such is not bad, what is creating harm to education is the form of politics takes in educational institutions and make it politicised. The situation became more tragic when politics directly interferes in the working of educational institutions.

Russ wrote, "One of the serious limitation of politicisation of education is the direct impact of political parties particularly their acts. The only way to keep students and educational institutions away from the existing crisis is the commitment on the part of the government to keep political interference out".[3] It further reports that the students taking part in politics should not be given admission or be expelled immediately.

In institutions the main cause of politicisation is the practice of favouritism which had a negative impact on teachers morale and teachers work involvement. In restructure of education, teachers argued that the everyday political actions of those who practiced favouritism tends to decrease the probability of their making sound educational and non-educational programmes and policy decisions.

The Principal: Politics of Favouritism

Practices Associated with Favouritism

According to recent findings big blause in Education Administration quarterly, 124 teachers focused on the role of schools, principals and practices of favouritism. They find principals as employing favourism in several decision areas when hiring. Principles were accused of conducting interview for jobs where decisions had already been made as well as hiring. Promoting and extending special favour to friends and relatives. Principals manipulated opportunities to attend country and state, seminars, workshops, conferences and noted problems of appointing uncertified teachers to positions in schools. There is inclination in principals to delegate authority to consult with selected individuals.

The problem of favouritism is seen in policy and rules, teachers reports favoured individuals had greater freedom and others don't have. They don't require to explain "Why they do? What they do".

Principles favouritism associated with resources allocation referred specially to decisions about finding materials, equipment and space allocation. They practiced favouritism in the distribution of work load responsibility. In the views of teachers favoured individuals were protected from bad classes and rough schedules." The friends of principal received excellent evaluations for teaching and general performance, while other teachers often received excessively negative evaluations. Even in disbursing information about school what is going on, teachers disclosed that principals informed some teachers and also accused many principals of sharing confidential information. Teachers also blamed principals for favouritism in the distribution of rewards for the work performance and special achievements of teachers.

Why Principals Engaged in Favouritism

Teachers indicated that principals engaged in favouritism for purposes of protection influence and control. On the whole, principals attempted to establish networks of exchange and even reciprocation i.e. two way exchange of favours for mutual benefit (Goulder, 1966), particularly with teachers and parents to induce 'legality' achieve goals, build power and solicite inside information.

Briefly, from the teachers stand point, important practice of favouritism by principals included status and/or power of significant others (school board members, superintendents, teachers and parents) rewards, conflict avoidance, avoidance of embarrassment, concern about public image precedent, friendship/ relations and advancement. As it is already indicated principals play politics to get work done. But when his action violate primary values (ideals, beliefs) of subordinates, consequences may result, both for the individual and the organisation.

The Effects of Favouritism on Teachers

Of the 124 teachers who described the impact of principal favouritism on their involvement in the class room, 61 per cent expressed a negative effect, 28 per cent suggested no effects, 11 per cent indicated positive effects. Generally they noted direct negative effects on teachers motivation, morale, satisfaction, sense of control, and teachers work load (time and energy) for class room preparation and instructions. Indirect negative effects were associated with the status of teaching as a profession and opportunities for professional growth.

According to the teachers, principals favouritism affected the 'quality' of administrative appointments, which in turn adversely influenced the class room. One teacher explained that the appointment of an incompetent science department chairperson with no proper knowledge of science or leadership ability affected all science teachers because they did not receive information and were not allowed to participate in curriculum development or attend science conferences. The positive effect of favouritism in that favoured teachers listened more carefully and asked more about things had more input to their situation, they worked hard to improve themselves.

The negative effects of favouritism on teachers involvement in the school were only slightly more than those effects on class room involvement. A total of 65 per cent of the teachers indicated a negative effect, 24 per cent no effect and 11 per cent described a positive effect on school wide performance. Teachers reported that principal favouritism affected their motivation and several quantitative (e.g. time) and qualitative (e.g. level of caring, interest) aspects of their involvement in extra curricular activities (function) sports and other programmes as well as routine duties and responsibilities they found themselves less willing and less interested to support school functions. They never go for extra work.....[4]

They have an attitude of resentment and rebellion against any decision or suggestion made by the principal. They think why to do anything you won't be appreciated further according to few teachers favouritism worked to reduce advancement opportunities and productive communication between principals and teachers and between favoured and unfavoured faculty. In situations of extensive favouritism, teachers described deep split, the formation of aliques (groups) and increased conflict in the school in which they worked.

As might be expected, the positive results of favouritism seemed to increase the favoured teachers involvement in the school. In general they try to do everything to please the boss to gain more favour.

The D.O.E. and Other Officers

These officers show politics primarily in decisions related to the hiring and retention of school personnel. They also show favouritism for friends/relatives who often did not possess proper degree, certificates or qualifications.

They are engaged in politics again because of some pressure from above (state government officials) friends and relatives. To maintain support and status among school personnel and community members. Again at the more abstract level the data strongly imply that the importance of exchange and reciprocation (you scratch my book and I'll scratch yours).

Effects

In the appointment of incompetent teachers/individuals (for principals post) the teachers, students have to pay dearly. The politicisation of education done by officers (educational) reduced opportunities for advancement which appeared to influence indirectly the teacher's orientation to the class room. Although they taught their students that education and hardwork were the way to achieve goals and status, teachers felt this formula really had not worked in their own situa ion. Even in one situation a favoured fellow of officer was not present on the interview day so the interviews were cancelled on that day. This type of behaviour really destroy the value and quality of education.

The Management

The management politics usually occurred in hiring and retention decisions of professional and non-professional school personnel. In short friends, relatives and those who have special standing in their communities (e.g. wealth, political ties) were hired or were allowed to influence hiring decisions for school system. In a few instances board members are seen to manipulate salary schedules for purpose of favouritism. Even in some schools or institutions donors also influence the activities going on in the school. Appointments of teachers and other non-teaching staff, passing of students and other co-curricular activities took place according to their views. And thus the school/institution loss there little bid of autonomy which it enjoys.

In the Blase research article in EAQ of the 56 teachers who discussed the impact of school management/board on teachers involvement in the class room, Sxity-one per cent indicated negative effect and 39 per cent no effect. Generally this effects on teacher's moral and motivation as well as the quality of teaching and administrative appointments, with a poor administrators appointment, one who is in consistent discipline policy,.... the whole problem of discipline falls on the teachers shoulders. This means more problem and less learning in the class room. Another teachers focussing on the implications of hiring incompetent teachers mentioned the extra burden of having to bring children to the appropriate academic and social level after they had spent the preceding years in the class rooms of incompetent teachers.

Other class room effects included constraints on teachers instructional methods, 'fear of voicing opinions' on potentially controvercial (*Educational Administration Quarterly*, May, 1988) subject related topics, and unwillingness to take proper disciplinary action with students connected to board/management/officers or principal. On this some teachers explained that since advancement opportunities were for closed friends, there is tendency to reduce involvement in the extracurricular programme and in work activities and events outside the class room.

Categorisation of the data into feeling states yielded the following results:

Anger states, 68 per cent; depresssive states; 16 per cent and anxiety states 16 per cent.

Parents and Community

Teachers disclosed that elite groups (wealthy), minorities and individuals with clout pressurised school officials for preferential treatment. Using political connections, parents often demanded favoured status for their children in academic, discipline and extra-curricular matters. In academics, for example, parents requested/demanded grade changes, passing a student and a special student placements (with a given teacher in particular programme). Parents also interfere related decisions, e.g., the quantity of home work, type of material and in functions. In the area of discipline parents frequently demanded favoured treatment for their children, despite standing policies and normative practices, especially about punishments incurred for violation of school rules. Some teachers indicated that community members with friends and relatives seeking jobs successfully influenced the selection of teachers and administrators.

All in all, as seen teachers accused school principals, for the most part (D.E.O. and management also) of acquiescing (accept silently) to parents and communative members with narrow self-serving political motives. Teachers further added that people in leadership make decisions based on the perceived power of the person making the request. The overall programme can suffer because an individual (parent) may be satisfied to the detriment of others.

Parents engaged in politics to promote special interests for their children, to control aspects of the curricular and extra-curricular programme, and to influence hiring decisions for school personnel, avoidance of embarrassment, exercise of powers, elitism, lack of rspect for authority and finally pragmatism.

Of the 44 teachers who discussed the political demands of parents (a/c to Blase) 64 per cent indicated a negative effect on teachers class room involvement, 32 per cent no effect and 4 per cent reported a positive effect (on morale). But sometimes parental interference in matters of students discipline was related to increased behavioural problems in the class room when administrators give in to parents.... students have an impression that they are beyond the disciplinary code.... thus opening rise to other students questioning their position within the school in regard to discpline. Similarly, parental infrusions in academic areas also precipitated negative reactions in teachers. Teachers find themselves in problems in both instructions and control in which parents interfered. Moreover, interference was linked to increased teachers stress, lower teacher morale, and a tendency for teachers to withdraw from the class room.

According to Blase the impact of parental behaviour on teacher involvement in the school, 77 per cent pointed negative effect, 18 per cent no effect, and 5 per cent saw positive effect on morale.

Teachers

A total of 72 teachers discussed the political behaviour of teachers, that they directly and aggressively exploited political contacts. It is not what you know but who you know is most important.

However, according to Blase the bulk of data indicated that teachers' political actions tended to be reactive; teachers "learned to survive" in situations precipitated by the actions and expectations of school officials and parents. In general it appears that teachers engaged in three types of political behaviour—ingratification, acquiescence and diplomacy—to gain favours from school officials, particularly principals.

Ingratification—is to flatter the school officials within the context of such motives, actions such as volunteering for committee work and praising administrators were considered as flattering or hypocritical.

Acquiescence— refers to overt behavioural compliance to the policies, mandates, directives and informal expectations of school administrators. Many teachers illustrate that many principals demanded "unquestionable obedience" as well as open display of support. There are some teachers who.... not only do not speak when they disagree but will actually support policies of the administrators for show to protect themselves from criticism.

Diplomacy— Teachers diplomacy was defined more positively. They stressed the importance of playing the game coupled with the purpose of achieving professional goals in a dignified manner. Consequently, teachers were tactful, patient and empathetic with school administrators.

According to Russ (1989) teachers engage in political actions linked for the following reasons: advancement, recognition/approval, avoidance of criticism, resource acquisition, evaluation, avoidance of responsibility, precedent, job security, avoidance and prestige. "A teacher will follow the game plan of the principal or current administration... to gain admission to inner circle."[5]

The Effects of Teacher Political Behaviour on Other Teachers

Of the 72 teachers who commented on how teacher actions contribute to politicisation, 72 per cent described negative effects on class room involvement, 22 per cent no effect, and 6 per cent positive effect on morale, for the most part negative effects were linked to teacher morale. Adverse consequences for work effort were especially obvious in situations in which the politics played by the principals was tied to resource acquisition or job opportunities for teachers. 'Teachers' said, "It would seem useless to try to do a good job in the class room if I would be passed over for a teacher who simply knew the right people." A total of 75 per cent of the teachers indicated negative effect on performance and involvement in the school, 19 per cent pointed to no impact and 6 per cent noted a positive impact on morale. It was evident for example that the practice of politicisation used to manipulate teachers was related to high levels of teachers acquiescence and ingratition. In turn they saw interpersonal animosities, jealousies and suspiciousness created by such practices and exacerbated by conflict between 'favoured' and 'unfavoured' teachers, as decreasing social cohesion in schools.

Campus Unrest

According to N.Venkataiah (1991) much of the unrest in the campus is due to political parties which encourage it to satisfy their own ends without any care for the larger interest of education or of the country.[6] Students have become divided into as many groups as there are political parties in the country. Election to university and college unions are fought among rival political groups. Without this backing of political leaders and unscrupulous politicians the situation would not have become so bad. If politicians are not interested in the campus politics, the academic politicians of the campus viz. some teachers who are supporters of the politics would approach them and involve them in the campus politics. In this race university student leaders are no inferior to teachers in supporting or opposing the political act in the campus.

One of the evil that effects the teaching profession today is politics among teachers. Politics in the form of trade union, direct involvement in the political activities, pressure groups among the regional and communal lines. All of them tend to put education at secondary place. Whatever is done in defence of their rights and privileges or to pressurize managements, or government for favours of various kinds. The growing threat being posed by teacher leaders or teachers politicians to the sanctity of the realm of education.[7] Gone are the days when teachers unions are bothered about the students welfare and cares for education. Today the activities are more or less anti-education and anti-student. Practically the whole of their time and energy is fritted away on politics and union activities.

The problem of political interference in the selection, posting and transfer of teachers is also seen equally serious affecting the teachers function and eventually education field as much as teacher's politics i.e. Those days were gone when Vice-Chancellors were appointed based on their intellectual brilliance or for their monumental achievements in the field of their vocation. Now a days V.C.'s are mostly appointed on blatantly narrow caste and political consideration. V.C.'s are who has got lots of favours from politicians for his appointment can't remain neutral and therefore will go out of the way to please them on occasions like recruiting the teaching or non-teaching staff.

Suggestions and views of different people for the control of politicisation of education is the main reason for the deterioration is universally known. The teachers remain busy in trade union activities which is stepping stone to early politics. Majority of teachers have become ambitious. This had led to indiscipline among teachers. And the entire academic atmosphere is politicised. They have no time for teaching and are in continuous conflict with management on the one hand and government on the other. Inspite of the fact that they are getting fairly satisfactory emoluments and other amenities from public exchequer at par with others. They have their representatives in the state legislature to protect their actions and voice their demands. But alas! there is no way to prevail them to do their sacred duty viz. teaching. There is no code of conduct for them and the result is growing indiscipline and falling standard. Therefore, a rightful step in this direction would be to abolish seats for teachers in Legislative Council of the state by repealing sub-clause (c) of clause (3) of Article 171 of Constitution or by enactment by Parliament under clause (2) of the said Article 171 of the Constitution whereas feeling of teachers have been expressed through their associations.

"Those who want to maintain *status quo* in politics, do not want teachers to take part in politics, because they feel that the teachers being enlightened persons will create political awareness, as they did in pre-independence days and bring about progressive change in the static politics based on ignorance or illiteracy of our population. In fact a teacher should have a major say in the politics of the country. That is why framers of the Constitution provided for teachers representation in the upper house of the states."

Students association from one of the northern states seems to be disguised with the state of affairs viz. "It is strongly felt by the general public that the greatest mockery that has brought the system to the death bed is the influence of politics and trade union in education. In a backward state like U.P. the teacher politicians had brought untold hardship to the students community."

Students and teachers should not take part in active politics. Much of the unrest in the campus is the result of instruction of politics. Political parties should refrain from using schools and colleges to their narrow partisan ends.

Depoliticisation of the academic and non-academic staff in the universities is necessary because they set bad examples for the students.

Educational institutions should not be allowed to become platform of political parties.

Introduce legislation to bar political parties involving students, teaching and non-teaching staff, like the neucle as free zone, the academic area must be made up of students with high academic record or performance.

Introduce legislation to ensure that politicians and political parties do not interfere in the educational field. This may perhaps mean to having formulate a code of conduct for politicians and political parties.

In the views of *'Sabera'* the use of students by political parties had already done enough harm to students. In this atmosphere, it is pointed out that political parties themselves should take a decision that educational institutions to be used exclusively for academic persuits. Political parties should stop misguiding the students. It is significant to note that political parties are the worst enemy of educational institutions and should treat them as holy places as in traditional India.

The Hindustan Times wrote:

"To restore the sanctity of educational institutions and to

preserve their independence it is imperative that party politics be banned just as they deserve to be banned from religious institutions and holy places."

Depoliticisation of educational institutions is necessary because vested political interests hamper with proper functioning of these centres of learning and also badly affect the task of maintaining educational institutions.

Depoliticisation of education which is long overdue should be given weightage in new educational policy, without this it will not be possible to clean educational institutions and to create smooth atmosphere for the academic activity. To check the involvement of teachers in active politics, some regulations have to be spelt out, that working teachers will not be eligible to contest elections will be by account the best remedy.

Alternatives

Looking at the conditions under which a university or educational institutions operates, conflict in every step inside and outside the institutions. In a domestic set up decisions will tend to be made by negotiations, bargaining, trade off, compromise and politics. It is such a political jungle that no one can be excused from it. There is always pressure from one corner to other. The administrator or individual can no longer sustain himself without groupism and these are certainly admirable and necessary or they will no longer suffice. The need of the hour indicate that one will have to learn a political creature. According to Dr. Derek (1992).

> "Educational leader is more politically intelligent, possess a high level of academic accomplishments and genuine commitment to strive for those ideals that education enshrines, namely to equip the learner with a set of skills, a quantum of knowledge and a socially sensitive frame of a mind that enable him to enhance the quality of life for himself and his community, so politics should be taken positively."[8]

There are many educational leaders which are academically well but as they are politically unfit, lack the necessary power to push their ideas and projects through can't able to bring the institution on the top of these all the efforts are in vain. But if these individuals are politically fit, know the power sources, they would possibly carry their plan to fruit on. They then also identified pressure groups against them and then sought out strategies possibly may neutralise them and may be won them, therefore—

Politics or politicisation of education is neither a bad thing nor a good thing. It all depends on the interest and intention underlying its use and the manner of its employment. The acquisition of power is certainly not an end..... in itself for the administer, teacher or individual. But it should be played (utilise) for the success of institution. The word 'politics' which itself concern with the obtaining of powers, utilising it, maintaining it, and enhancing it. According to Dr. Roy in his seminar (22.12.1992) it is said in a proper politicised atmosphere. Accountability can be achieved of course, it should not be dirty politics.

Role of Teachers to Overcome Politicisation in Education

It is to be agreed that politics should not be allowed in educational institutions, then the most crucial question is how to control it? It is sure that union is a major source of interference, therefore teachers or the pioneers should be awakened and unions should not be allowed to take a political form. It has been suggested in a daily *'SaDera'* that student union should not be banned, instead they should be formed with representation of the most meritorious students so that the academic faculties of the students should be guided in right direction.

There is yet another aspect which is to politicisation, is bureaucratisation of education. If politics hamper the development of education in one way the bureaucratisation affects it advesely in other way. This is because the bureaucrates look at education from a narrow perspective that administrative convenience. In this context it has been suggested that the bureaucrats should not be given the charge of educational institutions. As they are not able to promote academic interest.

Or a national policy to be adopted so that the school education upto +2 stage should not be polluted with narrow party politics. Some sort of socio-political projects (with the help of teachers) should be implemented at the secondary or higher secondary level to prepare future citizens.

Conclusion

According to Kothari Education Commission, 1966 "Educational institutions can no longer be information handling centres, but they have to be generation cells for creative, thought and imaginative action. They must provide thought and convert human beings into thinking organisations, generating new ideas. These new ideas should be such that they are directed towards solving the existing and future problems of the country and humanity in general. The education should be for the inculcation of basic human values, in creating a climate for the people to live enriching the quality of education and life."

The research described in this article points out that in the teachers view practices associated with politics negatively influence legitimate organisational policies, rules and procedures. The scope of politicisation (i.e. the number of different groups implicated in the phenomenon in a given situation) and the extent to which its practices influenced the thoughts, feelings, values and behaviours of individuals in the work setting were striking the practice of politicisation was sufficiently widespread to influence primary, political, social and cultural processes and structures of educational institutions.

More specifically, the finding from his study (Blase J) suggest that teachers are quite vulnerable to the use/misuse of power and political action by school officials; they perceived many such actions as having negative effects on critical qualitative and quantitative dimensions of teacher work involvement. Thus the study data emphasise the importance of power to the phenomenology of the educational setting by suggesting a significant link between how power is used by heads and its effect on the cognitive, affective and behavioural aspects of the work situation.

What emerges from this analysis is that politicisation itself is not bad. In fact it is a significant component in human development. But the way in which it has entered into educational institutions defeating the objectives of educational institutions has made the people conscious of the fact that it will have to be taken out from the educational institutions. In short we can say the negative effect of the politicisation of education on people is to decrease in motivation, work effort, low interest in extracurricular activities, low participation in communication and institutional activities, decrease in morale etc. The reason for this is politicisation played by the administrators under pressure from those with status, rewards from superiors, conflict avoidance, public image, friendship, relations, advancement, for the promotion of students, exercise of power, elitism, lack of respect for the institutions, pragmatism etc. authority. The politics is practised in decision making, hiring, promotion, appointments, termination, participation in programme and policy development, enforcement of rules, resource allocation, work load responsibility, evaluation, information, disbursement, recognition and rewards etc.

References

1. Blase, J.J., "The Politics of Favouritism", *Educational Administration Quarterly,* Sept. 1985.
2. Rudolph, I., *Education and Politics in India,* Delhi, 1970.
3. Russ, Q., "Politics of School Management", *Educational Administration Quarterly,* Vol. XXV, Feb., 1989.
4. "Towards Restructuring Education", *Views Survey* by NIEPA, Vol. I, 1991.
5. "Towards Restructuring Education", *Citizens Perspectives,* NIEPA, Vol. II, 1991.
6. Venkataish, "Campus Unrest", *University News,* Vol. XXIX, Dec., 1991.
7. Vasghase, P.P., "Evolution of the Concept of College Autonomy in India", *University News,* N. Delhi, Aug., 1992.
8. Derek, S., "Power, Politics and the Management of Education", A paper—CASE Baroda, 1992.

12

Socialistic Pattern of Society and Education

Article 30 of the Indian Constitution ask the state "to direct its policy towards ensuring that all the citizens, men and women equally, shall have the right to an adequate means of livelihood and that the ownership and control of the material resources of the community are so distributed as best to subserve the common good."

Article 40 directs the state "to take steps to organise Village Panchayats and endow them with such powers and authority as may be necessary to enable them to function as units of self government."

Article 43 of the Constitution directs the state "to secure by suitable legislation or by economic organisation or in other ways, to all workers, agricultural, industrial or otherwise work, a living wage, conditions of work ensuring a decent standard of life and full enjoyment of leisure, social and cultural opportunities."

Article 36 directs the state "to promote with special care the educational and economic interests of the weaker sections of the people and in particular of the scheduled castes and the scheduled tribes".[1]

Abovementioned directives of the state made significant reference to the achievement of socialistic pattern and fundamental requisites.

The broad objectives of the socialistic pattern of society are political equality, religious equality, economic equality and at the individual level to create new human beings by full growth of human personality.[2]

According to Shriman Narayan: "The basic objective of a Socialistic pattern of society would be the establishment of social and economic order based on equality of opportunity and on the social, economic and political justice."[3]

Socialistic pattern of society stress on equality and social justice. It includes individual refinement and social upliftment of the Indian masses and also include the removal of all the disabilities of the people on the basis of religion, caste, economic conditions, social and political status. The nature and complexion of the socialistic pattern of society established in India is determined by the idea of democracy and Sarvodaya. The democratic ideas of equality and justice are considered to be fully compatible with the ideals of socialism and so the protagonists of socialism in the country assert that this country will be able to rid her people of bondages of economic and social slavery if the political democracy is to lead to the economic democracy.

According to J.B. Kripalani: To define socialistic pattern of society is to try to define indefinable.[4] The socialistic pattern of society in its nature is essentially democratic, because the democratic way of life emphasises the political and economic democracy. The economic democracy ensures that each individual is free to realise the aspirations of his own economic well-being.

Indian Socialistic Pattern Based on Sarvodaya Ideal

Sarvodaya ideal represents the Indian concept of socialism. The Sarvodaya ideal seeks the fullest possible opportunity for the all-round development of the individual society. It lays stress on decentralisation of economic and political power. In capitalistic countries, the concentration of power is in the hands of the elite or big industrialists, while in the socialistic countries this concentration of power is in the hands of the party government. Indian brand of socialism embodied in Sarvodaya ideals believes in making the smallest unit of social life independent of Central control and the determiner of its own way of life based on sound ethical ideals. The stress on decentralisation and making the panchayat as an independent political and economic unit envisages an agrarian socialism. In such a socialism, the concentration of land holdings in a few hands would be eradicated. There would be equitable distribution of wealth in the village community and the distribution between landless and land owner would be wiped out. The Sarvodaya ideal believes in Socialism based on the ethical principles of life. The equitable distribution is not sought to create the craze for money even in those who are satisfied with their lot but to give them an opportunity to lead healthy, wholesome life which should be free from want. Thus Sarvodaya ideal envisages ethical socialism. It is not limited to the political, economic and social well-being of the people but it extends to whole of the life of the individuals. It is considered as a way of life. It seeks his individual development, development as a member of the society and nation and the enriching of the social and national life through moral and material progress.

Necessary Conditions for Socialistic Pattern of Society

In socialistic pattern the attainment of the objectives of equality and political justice are ensured. Such a structure will be possible when the following necessary conditions are fulfilled—

1. Equality of opportunity in social, political and economic sphere.
2. Every individual's right to work would be recognised and a living wage to all able citizens is ensured.
3. Production and all physical and natural resources in the country shall be effectively controlled by the state.
4. The community, as a whole shall be the gainer by the resources of the country and no section, group or segment to the community will have an exclusive right over them.
5. The existing disparities will be liquidated and followed by more equitable distribution of wealth among various sections of population of the nation.
6. Systematic attempts to eradicate poverty to produce more wealth in the country.
7. The transition of the present community to the society on the socialistic pattern will be through peaceful and democratic methods.
8. Decentralisation of economic and political power.
9. Prefer the small scale and cottage industries to bring economic prosperity.

Education for the Socialistic Pattern of Society

To achieve socialistic pattern of society it would be extremely necessary that a silent revolution is brought about in the social order so that all inequalities, injustices and distinctions are eradicated and a social climate is created where justice, fair play, equality and a right to lead a life free from want, misery and poverty are the recognised principles of greatest value. At Avadi session of the Congress, Pt. Jawahar Lal Nehru said:[5] "The development of India as a great co-operative Commonwealth necessarily meant equality of opportunity and social justice for all." The task before the country to-day is to bring about the silent revolution so socialism may replace the evils in the society. The accomplishment of this task requires the assistance of education. How education can assist in the process of the establishment of the socialistic pattern of society needs some elaboration. Shriman Narayan considers that there are even basic principles underlying a socialistic society. These principles are:

1. *Full Employment and Right to Work*

The education system has to be planned and reoriented in such a manner that every citizen of the country gets employment and earns a wage for which he is entitled on the basis of his ability, scholarship or training. Education has also to inculcate a feeling of the dignity of labour.

Gandhiji's basic system of education was based on the ideals of labour by hand and the creation of a moral life where everyone has to seek his own good through his own efforts and this system would have brought the idea of Sarvodaya. The vocational bias in the courses of study and the diversification of courses are some measures which need to be taken to ensure employment.

2. *Maximum Production of the National Wealth*

The economic prosperity can be brought if education is geared to the task. The national wealth cannot be increased by illiterate, uneducated citizens. For this general education to all upto a certain age-level and scientific and technical education to all the talented are necessary. The educational system has to equip the poor to earn more wealth. It has to create ethical and moral climate in the country so that hoarding and concentration of wealth is despised but the production of more wealth for national welfare is keenly sought.

3. *Maximum National Self-Sufficiency*

The nation has to achieve self sufficiency in her production and a lack of self-sufficiency will always result in exploitation by others and the cause of socialism will greatly suffer. The education system has to equip the citizen to produce those material goods which are in dearth in the country. It has to seek a full and complete utilisation of the country's natural resources. It has to impart training to the youths of the nation to attain higher production by using modern techniques and methods of production of material goods.

4. *The Social and Economic Justice*

To ensure social and economic justice, every citizen of the nation should get opportunities for higher type of education. A talented person should not find economic or social factors standing in his way for higher education. Every institution should be open to all the citizens of the nation. The admissions should be based on the consideration of merit and of the utility of such education to the individual and to the society. Denying admission to anyone on the basis of caste, religion, region or colour is the denial of social justice.

5. *Use of Peaceful, Non Violent and Democratic Method*

In India it is an evolutionary, peaceful process. Instead of violence it is sought to be brought through love. Instead of class conflict the self-sacrifice is considered as the correct means for its achievement. The educational system on democratic ideals can bring socialism much nearer. It has to create a moral development among the people so that they can understand the value of self-sacrifice. It has to create a hatred towards violence in the achievement of one's objectives. An education which does not only sharpen the mind but also sharpen the heart is required for the attainment of socialistic ideals. In practice, the general education needs to be emphasised together with the vocational and professional education.

6. *The Decentralisation of Economic and Political Power through the Establishment of Village Panchayats and Industrial Co-operatives*

For socialistic society, the necessity of starting at the village level is considered as that of supreme importance. This principle describe the mechanisation and the central control of power. The world today is relying more and more on machines and to talk at such a time of hatred of machines is considered as putting the clock back. The believers in Sarvodaya ideal argue that in India the capital is scarce and labour is abundant. If a machine casting a huge amount replaces the labour it will increase unemployment and will thus be undesirable.

For a sound national economy both the cottage and the heavy industries are needed. The cottage industries are needed to provide employment to the people and to boost the economy at village level. The mechanisation is necessary to construct heavy equipment for big projects like building dams, constructing canals, manufacturing heavy electrical mechinery and weapons for defence, etc. In fact education has to fulfil two fold tasks. It has to prepare the people for labour in cottage industries and for using the product of cottage industries by imparting proper training and inculcating the right spirit of nationalism and socialism. Secondly, it has to create a respect for machinery which helps in higher production, better standard of living and in the increase of national wealth without harming the cause of labourer and the farmer.

7. Unto This Last

Shriman Narayan feels accordance with Gandhiji's ideal of considering last man as that requiring our first concern. In a socialistic society the last is given first, means that the lowest of low persons lot should be first of all improved and that the movement for improving the living conditions should be set a foot. Gandhiji himself started with the upliftment of the Harijans who were at the lowest rung of the social ladder in our country.

Education helps in improving the status of down-trodden individuals. By opening the avenues of enlightenment he may be led to realise that his proverbial poverty has nothing to do with his 'Karma' and his low status is not based on any religious doctrine but on a dogma. This realisation will enable him to get his rightful place in the social order. This education will help him to improve his economic status and it will be helpful in freeing him from the shackless of backwardness.[6]

In many sociological and educational studies it is observed that education has a powerful influence in the socio-economic improvement of different classes of society. Who have an ordinary education background, accept education as an important instrument leading to the attainment of fair jobs but a vast majority who are highly educated and professionally qualified, have realised that it is education which has set them on the platform of socio-economic improvement. We can add here that education should inculcate the higher caste people a realisation of their duty towards the low and downtrodden. It should also free them from religious dogma and should encourage them to strive for social reforms. The educational system which envisages the improvement of the low and downtrodden should be encouraged.

Jai Prakash Narayan expressed his views in this regard at a public meeting at Madurai in July 1964 thus "Socialism is a way of life based on certain cultural, ethical and spiritual values. It seeks to create a social order founded on individual freedom, equality of opportunity and followship of men."[7] In our country it is hoped that socialism or socialistic pattern of society will truly be established only when our social and moral values have been transformed through the right kind of education by means of the various media of communication. The good education will provide to the nation honest, cultured, self-sacrificing and duty-bound citizens who will be real assets to the nation. They shall bring social reforms and establish an economic order where the disparities will be minimum.[8] They will work for national good and add to the nation's wealth but will not concentrate wealth in their individual accounts. The ethical ideals will always be their guide-post.

References

1. *Indian Constitution*, Govt. of India, 1950.
2. Jag Pravesh, *India's Socialistic Pattern of Society*, Metropolitan Book Co., Delhi.
3. Shriman Narayan, *Principles of Gandhian Planning*, Kitab Mahal, Allahabad, 1960.
4. Kripalani, J.B., "Congress Goal of Socialism still Nebulous," *The Sunday Standard*, May 3, 1964.
5. Pandey, Prem Narayan, *Education and Social Mobility*, Daya Publishing House, Delhi, 1988.
6. Gadre, Kamala, *Indian Way to Socialism*, Associated Publishing House, New Delhi, 1966.
7. Mukerji, D.P., *Diversities*, People's Publishing House, 1958.
8. Rosen, G., *Democracy and Economic Change in India*, Vohra Publishers, Bombay, 1966.

13

Religious and Moral Education

The National Policy Education (NPE) (1986) expressed a great concern over the erosion of moral values. It strongly emphasised that the "curriculum should be readjusted in such a way as to make education a forceful tool for the cultivation of moral and social values."[1] According to Ravindranath Tagore, "Education means enabling the mind to find out that ultimate truth which emanicipates us from the bondage of dust and give us the wealth, not of things but of inner light, nor of power but of live, making this truth its own and giving expression to it."[2] Education, thus means both the acquisition of knowledge and experience as well as the development of skills, habits and attitudes which help a person to lead a full and worthwhile life in the world.

Education is a force for the development of religion. Religion must form the basis of any education worth the name and that education with religion omitted is not really education at all. Today it is the conviction of an increasing number of thoughtful people that education if, it is to produce and maintain a high degree of civilisation and to safeguard against periodical lapses into barbarism, must be based on religion.

What is 'Religion'?

'Religion' etymologically means something that helps man to man. The word 'Dharma' which is very well known and generally recognised as a synonym of 'religion' mean many things like duties, responsibilities, ceremonies, customs and code of conduct. If every educated Indian knew and understand the guiding principles and spiritual values of religion, it would be the greatest advantage for him as 'individual' or as a member of the 'nation'.

What is Morality?

Moral values particularly refer to the conduct of man towards man in various situations in which human beings come together in the home, in social and economic fields and in the life of the outside world generally. It is essential that from the earliest childhood, moral values should be inculcated in us. We have to influence the home first. Habits, both of mind and body, formed in the early years at home, persist and influence our life afterwards. Good manners are a very important part of moral education. When good manners set they will impose a proper restraint on us and remove harshness in our words and rudeness in our behaviour and like the oil they helps to keep the machine of human society running smoothly. If our students learn about the integrity in their early years, they are not likely to go wrong later on. Therefore, every effort must be made to teach the students true moral values from the earliest stage of their educational life. *'Psychology of the Child and Curriculum'*[3] published by NCERT in 1983 has listed the following important moral qualities which need to be developed in children:—

1. Honesty in words and deeds
2. Truthfulness
3. Self-respect and desire to respect
4. Righteousness
5. Self-control
6. Duty consciousness
7. Compassion.

We have to lay special stress on the teaching of moral, religions and spiritual values. Being moral the students will be able to understand the principles of right and wrong and act in the right way. Being religious the students will be having a belief in the supernatural powers of god.[4] It also refers to performing a certain type of worship. It is not logically necessary for a moral person to go to a place of worship and have faith in religion. One could be moral without committing one-self to any religious faith. A religious person may not necessary be a moral person. Saints and seers have always stressed the importance of moral values and consequently of a clan life—life free from selfishness and greed.[5]

Methods of Imparting Moral Education

There are two important methods of imparting moral education—

1. Direct Method, and
2. Indirect Method

The *direct method* of moral education refers to the deliberate and systematic attempts made by the teacher to teach morality as a subject. It includes regular class-room instruction and discussion.

The *indirect method* of moral education implies morality through doing good acts and learning moral values through participation in social service activities. It also implies emphasising moral values during the course of teaching various subejcts.[6]

Religious and Moral Education at Different Stages of Education

The following suggestions merely indicate a broad framework of instructions in religious and moral education at different stages of education:

Elementary Stage

1. Assemblies for worship at the beginning of the day. According to Skinner, 'The school assembly must have certain characteristics if it is effective.'[7]
2. In the syllabus of language teaching simple and interesting stories about the lives and teachings of prophets, saints and religious leaders.
3. The interest on the child may be aroused by the use of audio-visual material especially good quality photographs, filmstrips and coloured reprints showing great works of arts and architecture closely connected with the main living religions of the world.[8] Such material could be used in teaching of geography and social studies.
4. Two periods a week in the school programme should be set aside for moral instruction. In these classes the teacher should relate interesting stories drawn from the great religions of the world and explain broadly their ethical teachings. Dogmas and rituals of religion should be excluded from moral instruction.
5. The feeling of 'work is worship' should be developed in the child at the time of school programme.

6. All schemes of physical education and all forms of play in the school contribute to the building of character and inculcation of the spirit of true sportsmanship.

Secondary Stage

1. The morning assembly should observe two minutes silence followed by readings from scripture or great literature of the world.
2. Apart from regular class instructions in moral and religious values, suitable speakers may be invited to address the students on moral, spiritual and religious values.
3. Organise social service during holidays and after class hours. Such service should teach the dignity of manual labour, love of humanity, patriotism and self-discipline.[9] Participating games and sports should be compulsory and physical education should be a normal part of school programme.
4. Qualities of character and behaviour of students should form an essential part of the overall assessment of a student's performance.

University Stage

1. Students should be encouraged to meet in groups for silent meditation in the morning.
2. General study of different religions, moral conduct and code should be an essential part of the general education course in degree classes.
3. A post-graduate course in comparative religion and history of religion may be instituted.
4. A fairly long period of social service should be introduced by all universities. In the organisation and conduct of such service, considerable attention should be given to the learning and practice of moral, religious and spiritual values.

Effective implementation of above suggestions will create a proper atmosphere in our educational institutions, so that the students may trained not only technicians or professional experts, but also human and balanced citizens who can contribute to the happiness and well-being of their countrymen and of humanity as a whole.

Role of School and Teachers for Effective Implementation of Religious and Moral Education

A school can play an important role in the moral development of children. The most important agent in the school is obviously the teacher. It has been stressed again and again that nothing can be more effective and helpful in moulding the child's moral behaviour than the teacher's own moral behaviour.[10] Teacher can foster among children various moral qualities through the organisation of various curricular and co-curricular activities. In the teaching of different subjects like languages and social studies etc. teachers can stress moral qualities.

The teacher should establish and maintain clear standards of behaviour and encourage the students to behave towards himself, towards one another and towards the whole community in an orderly and considerate way. Every school should demand a certain standards of behaviour from the students. The teacher should develop a rational acceptance of these standards in his pupils and also the ability to discriminate right from the wrong.

Education as a Force for the Development of Moral Conduct and Code

Our society is suffering today from indiscipline, concomitant, frustration and drift, resulting in widespread disturbance and dislocation of life. All are due to the gradual disappearance of values of life, noble sentiments and lofty ideals. The only cure, seems to us is in the deliberate inculcation of moral and spiritual values from the earlier years of our lives. If we lose these we shall be a nation without a soul.

The term 'Moral', implies behaviour and the adjectives 'moral' and 'immoral' suggest behaviour which is acceptable and unacceptable. Moral education is not concerned with telling truth, paying ones debts or having fellow feeling, but it is concerned with the whole conduct of man. Good conduct consists in training our pupil to respect and care for his body or to search faithfully after truth or to appreciate rightly the beauty of the world around. 'Morals' include every virtue and every goodness in them. They envisage:

1. Realisation and practice of higher value of life.
2. Training of mind or will power.

3. Discipline of instincts.
4. Changing our instinctive behaviour.

Moral value particularly refers to the conduct of man towards man in various situation in which human beings come together in the home in social and economic field, and in life of the outside world. It is essential that from the earliest childhood moral values should be inculcated in a child. 'Moral' can not be 'taught' it can be 'caught'. In the family the child acts as others act; he thinks and feel as other members of the family do. If the parents are honest, truthful, hardworking, courageous, disciplined and industrious their children will also initiate them in their day-to-day behaviour. Morality, which is defined as right conduct is practical which must be expressed in behaviour and not in words. The aim of teacher or education is to bring his pupils to understand the difference between right and wrong, between socially acceptable good conduct and socially unacceptable bad conduct. It is in the school that the child learns to show reverence for all that is noble and to strive after truth and purity of thought, word and deed. The child learn the habit of labour, preseverance, self-control, courage, discipline which ultimately lay the solid foundation of moral virtues like truthfulness, honesty, conquest of brute passions, fair dealings, sincerity, justice, temperance, non-violence, fellow feeling and promote the social efficiency of an individual.

Moral Code

We can teach morality by the use of moral rules or moral code. The value which a society holds and in the light of value-judgement result in the formation of moral rules or as they are called, a 'moral code'. These rules are prescriptive. The laws of any society are a set of prescriptive rules which determine what is legally acceptable behaviour. The laws are there to protect the interests of the society against those whose behaviour is anti-social. The legality or any other form of behaviour is determined in the light of moral code.

An individual act is properly to be called moral only when a man or woman either deliberately chooses to follow convention inspite of a temptation to deviate from it, or decided not to follow convention but choose instead to do better than his society tells him to moral education first a greater recognition of the common humanity of young and old. What we have in common with our children is more important than the years separating us: second the fostering of identity; third, the exercise of power of choice at many levels and fourth a greater encouragement of inititative and of taking of responsibility. There is no morality without decisions that are personal. Morality is concerned with good and bad behaviour. It is a social phenomenon since it involves the evaluation of the consequences of our actions for other people and their actions for us. It is in the pursuance of moral code mainly that the ideas of good and evil, virtue and vice, arise and are recognised. A great part of the culture of humanity and most of the traditional values which continue to influence human conduct, have been shaped by religion, which is even today one of the most powerful forces in our society.

Each society, should develop a code of behaviour suitable to its own needs to provide itself with stability. The teacher will help to create and maintain proper atmosphere in his institution. The teacher must, however be carefully trained to the objective of inculcating moral and spiritual values through understanding and respect for all religions. The teaching of moral, religious and spiritual values in educational institutions is desirable. The content of such education in moral value should include a comparative and systematic study of the lives and teachings of great religious leaders and at later stages, their ethical systems and philosophies. The inculcation of good manners, social services and true patriotism should be continuously stressed at all stages. In the course of extra-curricular activities, learned and experienced persons may be invited to deliver lectures on inter-religious understanding. Educational broadcasts and group discussion may be organised to stimulate interests in the study of moral and spiritual values.

References

1. *National Education Policy* (1986), Government of India.
2. Tagore, Ravindra Nath, *The Religion of Man,* the Hipper lectures, George Allen and Unwin, 1930.
3. NCERT, *Psychology of the Child and Curriculum,* 1983.
4. Articles on Arya Samaj in the *Encyclopaedia of Religion and Ethics.*
5. Sister Nivedita, *Hints on National Education in India,* Udbodhan Office, Calcutta, 1950.
6. Dewey, John, *The School and Society,* University of Chicago Press, 1936.

7. Kumarappa, J.C., *Education for Life,* Hindustan Publishing Co., Rajamuhundry, 1937.
8. Goyal, B.R. (Ed.), *Documents on Social, Moral and Spiritual Values in Education,* National Council of Educational Research and Training, New Delhi, 1979.
9. Joshi, Kireet, *An Outline Programme of Value-Oriented Education and Relevant Pedagogical Suggestions* in Report of the Working Group to Review Teachers Training Programme, Government of India, Ministry of Education and Culture, New Delhi.
10. Mukherjee, R.K., *Social Structure of Values,* S. Chand & Co., New Delhi, 1969.

14

Sociometric Study

Individual exists as a member of a group. The ability to understand an individual often requires an understanding of how he functions within the context on the membership in various groups. A child is a part of a family, a classroom, neighbourhood and possible clubs.

The purpose of education is development of individuality of the child so that he can make an original contribution to human life according to the best of his capability. In order to enable a school to provide such experiences as well as develop the individuality, it is essential for the teacher to know and understand the child in relation to the group to which he belongs.

Learning is a function of the learning situation. Learning in a classroom depends upon a good deal on the structure and pattern of inter-personal relationship particularly pupil-pupil relationship existing at a given point of time within the group. Most teachers realise that individual's personal and academic growth can be affected adversely or favourably by his position in the group and that all pupils stimulate or thwart one another in many ways. A successful teacher is one who can understand the nature of the emotional aspects of the intra-group relations of students in a class. Class-room learning can be most productive if a group is better understood.

Nature and Definition of Sociometry

Helen Jennings, one of the pioneers in the field of Sociometric studies, describes sociometry as a device for a graphic and straight forward portrayal of the total configuration of relations among the members of a group at a glance, the main lives of communication and the whole telescope of attractions and repulsions among members of the group. She described this method as follows:

"Stated briefly, Sociometry can be described as a means of presenting simply and graphically the entire structure relations existing at given time among members of a group. The major lines of attraction and rejection is its full scope one made readily comprehensible at glance".

According to J.W. Best: "Sociometry is a technique for describing social relationship that exists between individual in a group."[1]

According to J.L. Moreno; "This is a particular way of measuring social behaviour that test to study the structure and development of the group."

According to Franze, "Sociometry is a method used for discovery and manipulation of social configuration by measuring the attractions and repulsions among individuals in a group."

On the basis of all these definitions we may conclude that sociometry is a technique for describing social relationships that exists between individuals in a group. In an indirect way it attempts to describe attraction or repulsion between individuals by asking them to indicate whom they would choose or reject in various situations?

Sociometric technique may help in understanding group dynamics in schools. It can help in understanding students as members of a group. Sociometry has evolved a system of concepts appropriate for investigating the depth structure of group.

Importance and Use of Sociometric Test

A sociometric test is a means of determining the degree to which individuals are accepted in a group for discovering the relationship which exists among these individuals as far disclosing the structure of the group itself.

Sociometric technique consists in asking each individual in a group to state with whom among the members of the group he/she would like to associate for specific activities or in particular situations. From the answers obtained the choices each individual receives are added to give him a sociometric score and the choices made between or among particular individuals are recorded.

These results are often depicted on a sociogram. By counting the number of times a child is chosen, we can discover the degree to which he is accepted by other members of the group. Some children will be chosen often and other less frequently. The results enable us to know who are each child's particular friends. We can see whether he has a great number of different friends or a few special ones and also whether the children he considers to be his friends, are the ones who particularly like him. The sociometric test reveals structure of a group as a whole. From the results we can see if it is made up of clique or whether it is well integrated. With the help of this technique we can also discover the leaders within the group and their particular followers.

We can also compare the sociometric structure with the help of results of sociometric tests. We can use sociometric results for the research purposes as well. It shows whether the children who work hard at school are highly accepted by their new companions or not. We can also find the results of introducing new children into the classroom group.

The most practical use of sociometric test is to help organise and arrange actual classroom group. If the sociometric test is administered periodically the teacher might be able to trace the growth of the social adjustment of children. The value of this technique is useful for understanding educational projects and for making necessary seating arrangements. The wide use of children's real choices in classroom organisations helps us to create a favourable classroom climate.

Importance of Sociometry in Educational Guidance

One of the practical use of sociometry is in individual guidance through sociometric device, that we can understand the individual as a member of the group which is one of the aim of guidance.

There can be a child who is highly selected on a sociometric test and tends to be rated high on socially effective behaviour characteristics and has been noted to make more satisfactory adjustments to his social environment. Contrary to it, those pupils who are isolated or rejected by their peers have been generally characterised as possessing socially undesirable behaviour characteristics or exhibiting adjustment difficulties in the social sphere. Sociometric studies conducted abroad have indicated that the individuals with lower sociometric status are likely to deviate in different undesirable directions. The isolates, neglectees and rejectees are possibly dangerous not only to themselves in terms of their future development as potential psychotics or misfits but also to society in terms of their drive for social domination to compensate for lack of social assimilation.

"Sociometry is one of the techniques which helps in understanding the group dynamics. It helps the investigator in making a clinical or mental health appraisal and can provide clues which help him in social living of the child."[2]

By administering a sociometric test teachers can identify who is popular, isolate, neglectee etc. Teachers or a guidance worker can help the pupil function satisfactorily in social or group situations. Otherwise growth of dis-satisfaction may result in conflict and anxiety and in extreme cases it may result in several kinds of personality problems—withdrawals, anti-social tendencies like truancy and delinquency.

Characteristics of Sociometric Test

Following are the main characteristics of Sociometric test:

1. The sociometry test reveals the structures of the group as a whole. From the results we can see if it is made up of 'Cliques' or whether it is well integrated. With the help of this technique we can also discover the leaders within the group who are their particular followers. And if we give sociometric test at different times, we can discover how the group structure and the individuals sociometric and personal relationship have changed.
2. In condition to supplying this basic information, the results of sociometric tests can be used in many other ways. We can compare the sociometric structure of various groups, for example one class with another, or a class group with a group in another setting.
3. The most particular use of sociometric test, is to help, organise and arrange actual class room groups. The value of this technique is useful for understanding educational projects and for making necessary seating arrangements.
4. We can use sociometric results for children who work hard at school, are highly accepted by their companions

or not or whether these youngsters whom the staff judges to be best adjusted are the one's whom the other children particularly like. We can also find the results of introducing new children into a classroom rounds, or removing some of these who have been difficult.

5. By putting question such as 'Name the two pupil you want to play this game' with, 'Whom would you like to sit next to?' etc., will be possible for the teacher to elicit some of the information necessary for grouping pupils effectively.
6. Another important advantage of this method is that the teachers can select cleavages which reflect social standards among members of a group, cleavages arising out of race, religion and socio-economic status have deep roots. To maintain perfect understanding and harmony, the teacher must work with others in and out of school.

Definition of Terms Used

Popular or Star

The member of the group who receives a large number of choices on a sociometric test is a popular. He is also referred as star when he gets highest number of choices.

Isolate

Isolate is the member of the group who receives no choice on a sociometric device i.e. they are not chosen by any of the pupils in the class and they do not have any opportunities for interaction. He is physically a member of the group but psychologically isolated.

Neglectee

Neglectee is the member of the group who receives usually few positive choices. Neglectee is also referred to as a 'fringer' (as he is located on the fringes of the group) by some investigators.

Rejectee

Rejectee is the member of the group who receives negative choices. The rejectee can be identified only if the sociometric tool permits negative choices.

Clique

The term 'clique' signifies a sub-group within the large group. A sociometric clique is said to be formed when a number of members choose each another on the same sociometric criterion, and give few choices to members outisde their closely knit sub-group.

Cleavage

The term refers to a lock of sociometric choices between two or more sub-groups. The most obvious example is the choice pattern of boys and girls in a class. Thus in a co-educational class girls may choose girls and seldom choose boys. This is termed as sex-cleavage.

Mutual Choices

Mutual choice is the selection of two individuals by each other. Mutual choices often represent strong loyalties specially among adolescents. As long as the relationship is based on socially desirable aim it serves the important purpose of helping the individual learn about himself. But when mutual choices serve less beneficial purposes, often members of the group can be introduced into the relationship or members have to be separated.

Sociogram

Findings obtained by means of sociometric technique can be shown graphically in the form is known as a Sociogram. A choice may be represented by a single pointed arrow, a mutual choice by an arrow pointing in opposite directions. Rejections may be represented by dotted lines. Reciprocal or mutual choices, cliques and cleavages within a group can be very well identified by having a look at the sociogram.

Much can be discovered about individual pupils and about a group as a whole by having pupil rate or appraise each other. Thus sociometry is one of the techniques used to reveal group structure by showing preferences that persons in the group have, for each other, and the way in which individual persons are chosen as preferred or ignored or rejected.[3]

Objectives of the Study

The following objectives were formulated for the present study:

1. To find the sociometric status of students of class XI.
2. To find out the star or popular in the class.
3. To find out the neglectee.
4. To find out the isolate.
5. To study the nature of relationship among the students.
6. To prepare guidance programme to improve group relationships.

Administration of Sociometry Test

The effectiveness of sociometric test is highly dependent on the teacher who uses it. Sociometric techniques are of most value in classroom where the teacher has maintained a generally informal classroom behaviour. The direction should include the specific manner in which students are to record their choices. The sociometric test questions can be presented in various forms in the classroom. The questions may be in written form; one copy for each child and may be written on the black board or presented orally. Whatever form is used separately or in combination, the students need to be able to record his choices on a sheet of paper or index card. The test should be administered so that each individual's preferences are kept confidential otherwise it may serve to widen the tension between some pupils and their classmates. Teacher must be careful not to violate the confidence of his pupil.

1. Sample

The pupils numbering 27 of class VIII of a public school comprised the sample for study.

2. Tool

To study the group structure of class, a questionnaire of five questions was prepared by the investigator. This test was administered to the students in a group situation to collect the data on their social acceptability. The questions were used as a criterion for making a choice. The number of choices each student received on each criterion determined the degree to which he/she was accepted by his/her classmates.

Tabulation and Data Analysis

After taking the sheets, the results of the sociometric test were tabulated and presented in the form of sociogram. The sociometric test was developed. The numbers in the table indicate the students on both sides. The count was made of the choices and rejections and the total written below.

Formation of Sociogram

For construction of sociogram each student is represented in the form of circle on paper and choice of one to other is represented by an arrow. Mutual choices are shown by a line with arrow on both the sides. One who receives most choices is shown at the center as most of the lines meet there and those receiving few choices are shown on sides. So the person at the center is less accepted by the group. Thus within the sociogram we can identify the star, co-stars, isolatee, neglectee and rejectee in the group.[4]

The pupil who got highest choice was the 'Star' of the class. The pupil who got no choices was named 'isolatee'. The pupil who got maximum dislike was called 'rejectee'. The pupil who got least choices was named 'neglectee'. A separate record was maintained of mutual choices and one side priority. There is also a clique in this group.

Interpretation of the Result

On the basis of analysis of sociometric study following facts are gathered:

1. Popular

On the basis of sociogram No. 1 we can say that No. 24 is the star of the group. He is most popular in the class. He has got 23 choices out of 29. He should be selected for leadership of the class in various positions to maintain discipline, to solve any problem, to organise some programme such as picnic, game, party, seminar etc.

2. Isolatee

In this test there is a student no. 2 who has not been liked by any one in the group. So it is suggested that the teacher should motivate him to participate in the co-curricular activities, in other group activities so that he may get maximum opportunities to interact with the individuals.

3. Neglectee

From this test we can say that student No. 5, 8, 14 are neglected by most of the students. They have got only 2 and 3 choices respectively. So we can say that these three students are neglectes.

4. Rejectee

In this group it is identified that student No. 11 is a rejectee as he has got maximum negative choices respectively.

5. Clique

An interesting character of this group identified is a clique. The term clique signifies sub-group within the larger group. Sociogram No. 3 tells us that a group of six students i.e. numbers 3, 9, 12, 17, 21 and 24 like each other. They form a clique in their group.

6. Mutual Choices and One Side Choice

In this group of 29 students, some students have mutual choices meaning they have selected each other. On the other side some students have one side choice i.e. they have not reciprocated friendship.

Group Characteristics and Suggestions

On the basis of findings of this sociometric test we can give some suggestions to improve group relationships.

1. The star should be given opportunities to utilize his leadership traits and his organising ability.
2. The teacher should motivate the neglected students to participate in group activities, social gathering, games etc.
3. The teacher should change the seating arrangements in the class so that rejected students come forward. He should develop self-confidence in them. He should guide them to make better adjustment in the group.
4. For isolatee students, teacher should make special efforts to enter him into group activities. He should be motivated to participate in co-curricular activities i.e. games, picnic etc. He should establish personal relationship to understand him psychologically and deal with his personal problems.

5. In class, the teacher should give more importance to neglected and rejected students.
6. On the basis of their similar activities the students should be divided into some other sub-groups so that they can work to the best of their capabilities. It will create in them a sense of responsibility and self-confidence.
7. The teacher should pay special attention to the student who have formed clique. He should instruct them to do some creative work, to arrange party, seminar, exhibitions, any kind of competition etc. He should keep them busy in some constructive activities.
8. The teacher should also guide the star pupil and second leader of the group. He should try to develop creativity in them. He should create such opportunities so that they can make maximum utilisation of their ability in social welfare and social activities.[5]
9. The students who have got 17 and 15 choices out of 29 should be given opportunities to develop their leadership. Their teacher should pay special attention at this point because in future they may come out as stars and prove to be better leaders.

Limitations of Sociometry

Sociometry has certain limitations and it can be misinterpreted:

1. Sociometry interpretation is hazardous unless the interpretee knows other information about members of the group.
2. Sociometry does not indicate the reasons for acceptance, non-acceptance or rejection. It simply identify the current group choice structure.
3. It is too often assumed that 'isloate' must be withdrawn and introvert. Isolates can be quite adjusted, but they might simply prefer their privacy. Similarly many unhappy individuals can be extremely popular in the same situations.
4. Popular in the situation does not necessarily imply equal popularity in another. The star in a physical education calss might not exist in another class.
5. Sociometry choices depend highly on the nature of the questions posed *e.g.* It is one thing to be asked to name

the person you would want to work within a class assignment. Questions such as—With whom you would like to work on an algebra assignment might find a different response if the assignments were changed to social studies.[6]

Suggestions to Improve Social Status of Neglectee, Rejectee and Isolates

1. Neglectee, Rejectee and Isolates should be provided leadership role in the class.
2. Due opportunities must be provided to make them busy in some or other group work.
3. Due attention should be paid on their participation in co-curricular activities.
4. Teacher must develop proper communicative rapport with them so as to motivate them to work in group and to raise their self-confidence.

Conclusion

Sociometric methods are means of determining the relationships existing among members of a group at a given time. Several methods have been found useful in determining each relationship.

(a) Any individual may be asked to name a limited number of people from within the group with whom he would choose to associate on the basis of a stated criterion.

(b) An individual may be asked to rate all the other members of this group using some predetermined scale.

(c) An individual may be asked to select those members in his group who show defined characteristics.

(d) Sociometric techniques have been found to be of use in promoting the social adjustment of pupil, in promoting common interests and skills of a group, in grouping people for various class activities, in measuring growth in group status and in detecting cleavages which reflect social standards among group members.

Questionnaire for Students

Name of Student—...

Name of School—...

Class—..

Age—...

INSTRUCTIONS:

Dear Students,

You are requested to write the name of student of your class from questions 1 to 4 according to your own choice. In each question write three names in order of your preference. In question 5 write the name of only one student of your class.

Q. 1. With which student of your class would you like to play?
(a)
(b)
(c)

Q. 2. Which student would you like to be the monitor of your class?
(a)
(b)
(c)

Q. 3. With whom would you like to study?
(a)
(b)
(c)

Q. 4. With whom would you like to eat food?
(a)
(b)
(c)

Q. 5. With whom would you not like to do any of the above activities?
(a)
(b)
(c)

References

1. Best, J. W., *Research in Education,* Prentice Hall of India Pvt. Ltd., New Delhi, 1986.
2. Good and Barr, *Methods of Social Research,* McGraw Hill Book Co. Inc., New York, 1952.
3. Jennings, H. M., *Sociometry in Group Relations,* Washington, American Council of Education, 1954.
4. Sukhia and Mehrotra, *Elements of Educational Research,* Allied Publishers Pvt. Ltd., New Delhi, 1966.
5. Wilkinson and Bhandarkar, *Methodology and Techniques of Social Research,* Himalaya Publishing House, Bombay, 1982.
6. Young, P. V., *Social Survey and Research,* Indian Edition, 1975.

15

Social Survey

Social survey is an oldest and popular technique for collection of information about the society or phenomena. Herodotus has mentioned about a survey of population and wealth in Egypt in 300 B.C. We read about the collection of economic statistics in Kautilya's *Arthshastra*. John Howard made a survey of the Prisons and collected information about the prison life by actually living in the prisons. Charles Booth made comprehensive study of the Community life of London and collected information about a wide range of socio-economic factors. In 1928 Eaton and Harrison compiled a Bibliography of social surveys and listed a total of 2775 Surveys completed upto 1927 in U.S.A. alone. Of this 154 were general and 262 specialised surveys. This indicates that main focus was shifted from collecting general information to small problemetic surveys of a single aspect.

Now small surveys for testing particular hypothesis are undertaken and more attention is being paid to detailed and closer study of behaviour rather than mere collection of mass data. Large surveys by private individuals and institutions become less frequent now. This is mainly because comprehensive data on many social problems like health, social security, crime, population etc. are collected and supplied regularly by government agencies. Instead of exhaustive, painstaking and time consuming survey of the old, we now have short, problematic studies most of which remain un-co-ordinated.

Meaning and Definition of Social Survey

The literal meaning of a survey is to take over some thing from a high place but it has come to be used as a term with specific cannotation of its own.[1] The term social survey indicates the study of social phenomena through survey methods.

According to Shelby M. Harrison, "A Social Survey is a comparative undertaking which applies scientific method to the study and treatment of current related social problems and conditions having definite geographic limit and bearing such a spreading of facts, conclusions and recommendations and will make them as far as possible the common knowledge of the community and a force for intelligent co-ordinated action".[2]

According to Herman N. Morse, "The Survey is in brief a method of analysis in scientific and orderly manner for defined purpose of given social situation or problem or population."[3]

Mark Abrams consider social survey, "as a process by which quantitative facts are collected about the social aspect of a community composition and activities."[4]

The sociologists look upon surveys' as away and a supremely useful one of exploring the field, of collecting data around as well as directly on the subject of study so that problem is brought into focus and points worth studying are suggested. It is confined to the study of immediate problems of society e.g. poverty, unemployment, delinquency, crime etc. Its field of study is geographically localised. The main purpose of survey is to prepare constructive programme of social research or removal of immediate evils. The facts collected in a survey may form the basis of further social research on the matter. They may result in formulation of a new hypothesis requiring further elaboration but it is not always the object of a survey.[5]

Fundamental Difference Between Social Survey and Social Research

Social survey and social research are indentical in nature in many respects. Both of them deal with social phenomena. The methods and the technique used in both of them are almost similar. Both are inter-dependent and are influenced by each other.[6] But there are some fundamental differences between the two which may be classified as under:

Social Survey	*Social Research*
1. Social Survey is related to specific person, problem or situation.	Social Research is related with general and abstract problem.
2. Social Survey is practical by nature.	Social research is theoretical in nature.
3. It is utilitarian in nature.	It is purely scientific in nature.
4. It results in a social reform, or a remedial measure for removing evils.	It results in formulation of new theories or discovery of new techniques or study or modification of old concept.
5. A hypothesis is not necessary for it, generally a Social Survey is undertaken without any hypothesis.	The social research is mainly concerned with the testing of hypothesis.
6. It may be conducted not for any interest in the topic but on payment from other interested parties.	Thrust for knowledge is the only incentive and its ultimate satisfaction is the only reward for a social scientist

Objectives of a Social Survey

Social survey may be organised simply by a need for administrative facts on some aspect of public life or be designed to investigate some cause effect relationship. The surveys may be motivated by a number of following objectives.

1. Provide Information

Most of the surveys are meant to provide information regarding practical problems for example in education survey we collect information about the number of institutions, primary, secondary, Higher Secondary and higher education, education level of parents, parents income, number of teachers male/female at different level etc.

2. Description of a Phenomena

Social survey may equally have a purely descriptive purpose as a way of studying social conditions relationships and behaviour.

No description of a phenomena would be accurate and complete unless we come face to face with it. Anthropological Surveys of small Communities and socio-economic surveys describing living conditions of the people of a geographical area may be cited as illustration of this kind. The purpose of these surveys is to collect general information and they are not meant to prove or disprove anything.

3. *Explanation of a Phenomena*

Many enquiries are aimed to explain rather than to describe, their function may be theoretical—to test some hypothesis suggested by sociological theory—or several practicals to assess the influence of various factors which can be manipulated by public action, upon some phenomena—but whichever be the case, the purpose is to explain the relationships between a number of variables. This is the theoretical importance of survey. Before we embark upon such surveys we must have hypothesis to test or a problem upon which we require some specific information to establish some casual relationship.

Subject Matter of Social Surveys

Survey method is very widely used in a number of disciplines. The subject matter of social survey depends upon the nature of information gathered. Campbell and Katona divided the subject matter into four broad classes:

1. Personal data,
2. Environmental data,
3. Behavioural data, and
4. Level of information, opinions, attitudes, motives and expectations.

Moser has divided the subject matter into four broad classes. These are:

1. Demographic characteristics,
2. Social environment,
3. Social activities, and
4. Opinions attitudes etc.

1. *Demographic Characteristics*

Information regarding such matters as family or household composition, material status, fertility, age etc., are some of the examples of this type of survey. This includes surveys about organisation and working of family and other social institutions.

2. *Social Environments*

A number of social actions are conditioned by the environment in which people live. It covers all the social and economic factors to which people are subject, including occupation and income as well as housing conditions and social amenities. A study of family relations would require information on the location and degree of contract with parents and in-laws. A survey of delinquents would be incomplete unless knowledge of their home and family environment is available.

3. *Social Activities*

This termed as behavioural data and mainly deals with the actions or behaviour of the respondents. Use of leisure, travelling habits, expenditure pattern, radio listening, newspaper reading, geographical or social mobility or pattern of voting are some of the illustrations of this kind of data.

4. *Opinion and Attitudes*

Opinion and attitude surveys are very common. They include attitude of a person towards any social, economic or political incident, institution or personality. In this group we can include the data regarding the level of information, opinion and attitudes of the people towards various social factors, their motives and expectations.

Besides the above classes, surveys may be undertaken to collect any other type of socio-economic, socio-political or Socio-psychological information that is not readily available from the official records and which can be had from the direct contact with the respondents.

Types of Surveys

Surveys may be classified into various types according to their subject matter, technique of data collection, regularity etc.

Classification on the basis of subject-matter has already been given in this chapter and following are other classifications.

1. General or Specific Survey

When a survey is conducted for collecting general information about population, institution or phenomena without any particular object or hypothesis it is known as a general survey. Such surveys are mostly undertaken by the government for supplying regular data on many socio-economic problems. Census of population every tenth year is a typical example of such a survey.

Specific surveys are conducted for specific problems or for testing the validity of some theory or hypothesis. These surveys are naturally more pointed and only such information which is directly related to the specific purpose is collected. Information gathered through these surveys is generally of very little value outside the problem under study.

2. Regular or Ad-hoc Surveys

Some surveys are regular in nature and must be repeated after regular intervals. For such surveys a permanent machinery for collecting information has to be set up. Most of such surveys are mainly economic. A survey of family budget, rural credit survey of family budgets, rural credit survey of Reserve Bank of India can be cited as examples. Such surveys are undertaken where continuous data is required to study the trend or the effect of time upon the phenomena under study.

Ad-hoc surveys are undertaken once for all. They may also be conducted in phases if the area of investigation is large, the whole survey being finished in two or more instalments. These type of surveys are undertaken mostly for testing a hypothesis or supplementing some missing information regarding any research problem.

3. Preliminary and Final Surveys

A preliminary survey is generally known as 'Pilot Study'. The purpose of this type of survey is to get the first hand knowledge of the universe to be surveyed. It helps to a person to get acquainted with the problem and the nature of respondents from whom the information is to be collected. These type of surveys are very useful in preparing the schedule or questionnaire and organizing the survey on proper lines. Final survey is made after the pilot study has been completed.

4. Census and Sample Surveys

In a census survey every single unit in the universe is to be contacted and information collected from him. In case of a sample survey only a small part of it is taken as representative and data collected from the whole universe. For example, in a study of smoking habit among the students of Udaipur, we may contact each one of the several thousand students to get the requisite information or a sample of few hundred may be taken and data so collected may be made applicable to the whole group. This survey is more popular because of convenience, time saving and low cost.

Planning a Social Survey

Designing, organising and conducting a survey is like establishing and running a business enterprise. Because it require technical knowledge, skill, administrative ability and specific experience or training in work similar to that being organised. An unplanned research work may entail a lot of fruitless labour and wastage of time, money and effort. Most of the unplanned studies fizzle out before they have reached their final stage because the researcher may find himself face to face with difficult problems which he had never thought and which is never prepared. *The Steps of planning a survey* are following:

1. Selection of the Problem

For selecting the problem some factors may be kept in mind.

(a) The problem should inspire the researcher.

(b) The problem should be allied with the chain of thinking.

(c) It may be old or new, should satisfy his sense of varity and purely scientific.

(d) The topic should be within manageable limits and not be too comprehensive. Vast subject of study may be unfit for real research work. It requires a real sense of humility and a definite control over temptation on the part of the research worker to confine himself to narrow topics.

(e) The topic should preferably possess some direct utility and practically feasible.

2. *Preliminary Preparations*

After the broad topic of study has been selected, certain preliminary preparations are essential. The researcher must acquaint himself with all the material that is available on the matter. This may consist of written texts, research work and unpublished information. He should find out the persons who have conducted research are special study of the problem, should contact them, discuss with them the problem, their findings, technique followed by them and the difficulties faced. This early preparation will make him more equipped and better suited to tackle the problem under study.

3. *Selection of Sample*

Social phenomena is very vast. It is practically impossible to contact each person. Therefore, a sample is generally drawn from amongst the people about whom the study has to be made. The most essential feature of a good sample is its representativeness. The sample must be capable of yielding accurate and reliable picture of the total. It should include as fully as possible the qualities and attributes of the universe and must be simple and easy to be drawn. For example, if it is proposed to conduct a survey of the educated tribal women of Banswara district, we must know the total mumber of educated tribal women in Banswara district. A list of all cases of universe, knows as source list, is prepared and the sample is drawn according to systematic sampling methods. Even after a sample has been drawn it should be tested by internal and external checks.

4. *Decideing the Method of Study*

Different kinds of methods are used in social research. Each method has its own advantages and limitations. The research worker should, therfore, decide in the very beginning as to what particular method is going to be used. In selecting the method he should take into consideration not only the suitability of the method but his own knowledge also. More than one method may be applied but a prior planning of the same is essential.

5. Nature of Information to be Collected

Social phenomena is generally very complex and influenced by a number of variables. It is, therefore, essential to decide before hand what information is to be collected. Questionnaire and schedules are generally prepared for this purpose. They contain certain set of questions that are to be asked from the informants. Questionnaire and schedule brings uniformity and thus introduce objectivity in the study. A proper drafting of these documents is very essential. Any slip in the language may distort the meaning and may create anamolies in the replies. Required information should be complete. After the study has been completed, if some important information has been left out it will require the same quantity of labour and effort again to gather it. Therefore, enough care should be exercised in this respect.[7]

The researcher has to make a plan, however short and sketchy, to get an idea to what information is to be collected. It may be in the form of interview guide, giving broad headings upon which questions are to be put or only a summary of information is to be collected.

6. Organization of Survey

If it is a quantitative survey, a good deal of organisational work is required for successfully conducting it. A number of field workers may be required. If they are not trained they must be given necessary training. Proper arrangement should be made for checking and supervising their work so that they may not give false reports. After the report has been received, it has to be edited. A thorough checking of the forms has to be undertaken. After this the data has to be classified, coded and presented in forms of tables.[8] It is subjected to various kinds of analysis and ultimately conclusions are drawn proving or disproving the hypothesis. All this organisational work should be pre-planned. The researcher may put up his own organization or may take the help of some already existing professional body. If the project is quite big and likely to take enough time, it is generally more useful to set up ones own research organisation.

7. Report

After the data have been analysed and generalization are drawn. These generalisations are often put in the form of a report. If the survey has been undertaken at the instance of a third party, care should be taken to see that all the information demanded by him has been supplied. At such times the surveyor may give his own opinion as well as suggestions regarding the problem under study. The proforma of report to be submitted should be decided before hand as it is very helpful in deciding the nature of information to be collected and the form in which it is to be analysed.

8. Protesting or Pilot Study

Even after a theoretical preparation has been made some sort of trail survey is necessary to gain specific knowledge of the subject and get an idea of the various problems likely to be faced in the course of the survey. These trial surveys are variously known as pilot study, protesting, test tube survey etc.

In protesting the same procedure is followed as is to be adopted in actual survey. Every detail is to be followed with some precision. The number of cases to be included in the pilot study. Sample differs according to the nature of survey. Generally 100 or more cases are taken. Sometimes less than 100 cases are considered enough.

In case if any schedules or forms are to be used, they must be given a trial in the pilot study. The pilot study sample should be as far as possible representative of the main sample and must include from all the strata. Necessary amendments should be made in the questionnaire, method of study, the sample drawn and other plans of field organisation. If a substantial change has been introduced as a result of the pro-testing a second or even a third pilot study may be essential.

9. Cost Estimates

Even survey entails some financial expenditure which varies from survey to survey, according to the scope and size of survey, time required, nature of information to be collected. A prior estimate of financial requirement is absolutely essential. A hurried start without a definite plan may result in financial bottleneck in the advanced stage of the survey and may even result in utter waste of time and money previously employed on it.[9] The resources also should be pre-planned and definitely ascertained.

In preparing cost budget all the necessary items of expenditure may be taken into account. They may include such item as purchase of books, stationery, files, payment to be made to staff both clerical and field workers, conveyance and travelling expenses as well as other charges incidental to the survey work.

A reserve of 10 per cent for any contingencies must be made. Expenditure to be incurred on report must also be taken into account. No hard and fast rules can be framed regarding the expenditure likely to be incurred. It entirely depends upon the nature of the survey and the circumstances in which it is to be carried out. The general method is to divide the survey into following three parts:

(a) Planning the survey and drafting questionnaire and interview schedule.
(b) Investigation in the field, collecting data, editing schedules.
(c) Coding, tabulating analysis data and writing report.

Formation of equal and correct budget is very important to work efficiently.

10. Time Estimates

In planning of any study time factor plays a dominant role and has a great importance. In telegraphic or telephonic surveys the report has to be given as quickly as within 48 hours. This type of survey generally deals with attitude and opinion polls about some problems of immediate importance *e.g.* chances of a particular candidate in election. In such a case information may be collected on telephone or actual interview is despatched telegraphically to the head office. Day and night work has to be done to tabulate the information collected and bring out the result in time.

No hard and fast rules can be given for calculating the time to be taken in survey. This depends upon the nature of information to be collected, the number and efficiency of the field workers, co-operation of the respondents, length of questionnaire or interview schedule, the geographical distribution of the informants, arrangement for despatch, tabulation, analysis and printing of report etc.

References

1. Campbell, A. & Katona, G., *Social Survey: A Technique for Social Science Research.*
2. Shelby, M. Harrison, *A Bibliography of Social Survey.*

3. Morse, H.N., *The Social Survey of Town and Country Areas.*
4. Mark, Abram, *Social Survey and Social Action.*
5. Donald Ary, *et al., Introduction to Research in Education,* Holl Rinehart and Winston Inc., New York, 1972.
6. Black, J.A. & D. J. Champion, *Methods and Issues in Social Research,"* John Wiley & Sons, 1997.
7. Englehart, M.D., *Method of Educational Research,* Rand McNally & Co., Chicago, 1972.
8. Fox, J. David, *The Research Process in Education,* Holt Rinehart and Winston, New York, 1969.
9. Kaul, Lokesh, *Methodology of Education Research,* Vikash Publishing House, New Delhi, 1984

Bibliography

Alexander, K.C., *Caste Mobilisation and Class Consciousness* in Frankel, F.R. and M.S.A. Rao (eds.), "Dominance and State Power in Modern India: Decline of a Social Order, Vol. 1, Oxford University Press, Delhi, 1989.

Bhatt, B.D. & Sharma, S.R., *Sociology of Education*, Kanishka Publishing House, 1993.

Bremback, C.S., *Social Foundation of Education: A Cross Cultural Approach*, John Wiley, N.Y., 1966.

Brown, F.J., *Educational Sociology*, Prentice Hall Inc., 1961.

Chaube, S.P., & Chaube Akhilesh, *Philosophical and Sociological Foundations of Education.*

Cook Lloyd Allen & Cook Elainef, *A Sociological Approach to Education*, McGraw Hill, New York, 1950.

Damle, Y.B., *Reference Group and Mobility in the Caste System* in Silverberg, James (ed.) "Social Mobility in the Caste System in India", Mouton Pub., The Hague, 1968.

Dowse Robert E. & Hughes, John A., *Political Sociology*, John Wiley & Sons, New York, 1972.

Ghosh, Bimal, *Profiles of Social Change*, Oxford & I.B.H. Publishing Co., New Delhi, 1979.

Illich, Ivan, *De Schooling Society*, Harmondsworth, Penguin Books, 1973.

Kuppuswamy, B., *Social Change in India*, Vani Education Books, New Delhi, 1986.

Midwinter, Eric, *Education and the Community*, John Wiley & Sons, New York, 1975.

Malik, S.C. (ed.), *Determinants of Social Status*, Indian Institute of Advanced Study, 1986.

N. Jayaram, *Sociology of Education in India*, Rawat Publication, Jaipur, 1950.

National Policy on Education 1986, Govt. of India, Ministry of Human Resource Development, New Delhi, 1986.

Olsen, M.E. *The Process of Social Organisation*, Holt, N.Y., 1968.

Paliwal, M.R., *Social Change and Education*, Uppal Publishing House, New Delhi, 1984.

Parsons, Talcott, *The Social System*, Tavistock Publishing, 1952.

Programme of Action, *National Policy on Education 1986*, Government of India, Ministry of Human Resource Development, New Delhi, 1990.

Report of the Committee for the *Review of National Policy on Education*, Government of India, 1991.

Shah, A.B. (ed.), *The Social Content of Education*, Essays in Honour of Prof. J.P. Naik, Allied Publishing, 1978.

Sharma, K.L., *Social Stratification in India, Issues and Themes*, Sage Publication, New Delhi, 1997.

Shah, B.V., "Sociology of Education—An Attempt at Definition and Scope," *Sociological Bulletin* (Vol. XIV, No. 2), Sept., 1965.

Sharma, S.N., *Philosophical and Sociological Foundations of Education*, Kanishka Publishers, Distributors, New Delhi, 1995.

Singh Yogendra, *Sociology of Social Stratification* in a survey of Research in Sociology and Social Anthropology, ICSSR, Vol. II, Satvahan Publications, New Delhi, 1985.

Smeser, Neil J. (ed.), *Sociology: An Introduction*, John Wiley, NY, 1967.

Social Stratification and Change in India, Manohar Publishers, Delhi, 1977.

Srinivas, M.N., *Social Change in Modern India*, University of California Press, 1966.

Thapar, Romila, *Social Mobility in Ancient Indian Society* in Sharma, R.S. (ed.). "Indian Society, Historical Probings," Peoples Publishing House, New Delhi, 1974.

Tumin, Meivin M., *Social Stratification*, Prentice Hall, New Delhi, 1969.

Varshney, Uma, *Education for Political Socialisation*, Meenakshi Prakashan, New Delhi, 1983.

Westby, Gibson D., (Ed.), "Social Foundations of Education: Current Issues and Research," *Free Press*, New York, 1967.

Worsley, Peter & Others; *Introducing Sociology*, Penguin Books, England, 1970.

Young, Kimball and Mack, Raymond, W., *Sociology and Social Life*, American Book Co., NY., 1962.

Index